W. Kelso Morrill, Dean of Students, The Johns Hopkins University, has been an outstanding lacrosse player, coach, and referee. In 1932, when Dr. Morrill was attack coach for the Johns Hopkins team, it represented the United States in the Olympics at Los Angeles and defeated Canada, the other contestant. He became head lacrosse coach in 1936, and, under his guidance, The Johns Hopkins University lacrosse team in 1941 won both the intercollegiate title and the open championship.

THE GAME AS FIRST PLAYED BY THE INDIANS

LACROSSE

W. Kelso Morrill
The Johns Hopkins University

REVISED PRINTING

THE RONALD PRESS COMPANY • NEW YORK

This book is dedicated to
John N. Richardson
and to my son,
William Kelso Morrill, Jr.

FOREWORD

It is doubtful if any treatise on sport has ever been presented by anyone more eminently qualified to do so than Dr. W. Kelso Morrill of the Johns Hopkins University. Dr. Morrill—student of the acknowledged dean of American lacrosse coaches, William (Father Bill) Schmeisser; regular member of championship Hopkins teams; Assistant Coach and later Head Coach of championship Hopkins teams—possesses the intimate knowledge of lacrosse gained only through close contacts with all phases of the game. His background in mathematics reveals itself in the fine analytical manner in which he portrays each situation in the game. The book can be used with real profit by beginner, finished player, and coach of lacrosse.

It is a privilege and a pleasure to introduce LACROSSE to lacrosse enthusiasts. Dr. Morrill imparts to this book that fine spirit possessed only by the true sportsman. It is hoped that this spirit will pass on to the reader.

ALBERT A. BRISOTTI
Former Editor, *National Collegiate
Athletic Association Lacrosse Guide*

PREFACE

The purpose of this book is to give to those unfamiliar with lacrosse a detailed description of the game (how it is played and what the individual players are expected to do). To player and coach alike it should prove interesting and valuable.

Lacrosse is one of the few games in which the individual players have so much opportunity to think for themselves. At some time in every contest, each player becomes the master of a particular situation. In order to become a good lacrosse player, two things are important: expert stick handling and a thorough knowledge of the game. Each takes practice, hours of practice, both physical and mental, hours of practice in catching, throwing, turning, cutting, dodging, and shooting. Things which seem so unimportant to the beginner and so boring to the veteran—such as learning how to turn after catching the ball, when to pass, when to cut, how and when to dodge—are fundamental.

Lacrosse combines the beauty of team play with the thrill of individual skill. It contains the rough and tumble of football, the speed of basketball, the endurance of a long-distance runner, and the finesse and skill of hockey. It calls for nerve and strength, and also adroitness and intelligence. It has been rightly called the "fastest game on two feet."

Lacrosse originated with the Indians and is one of the few purely American sports. Its history is colorful. Hence, I have included in the book a brief section on the history of lacrosse. For some of the facts I am indebted to W. G. Beers and his book *Lacrosse, The National Game of Canada* and to Cyrus Miller, who in 1904 helped to organize the present Intercollegiate Association.

I have dedicated this book to John N. Richardson, long-time friend and lacrosse enthusiast, and to my son, William Kelso Morrill, Jr., an outstanding lacrosse player at the Johns Hopkins University and for three years an All-American.

I also wish to express my appreciation to Mrs. Charles LaPointe for her aid in the typing.

I hope that this book will serve a useful purpose for both coach and player and that, because of it, more people may learn to play this grand old game, lacrosse.

W. KELSO MORRILL

Baltimore, Maryland
January, 1966

CONTENTS

LEGEND

●   THE BALL

○   AN ATTACK PLAYER

②   A SPECIFIC ATTACK PLAYER

③   AN ATTACK PLAYER WITH THE BALL WHO INITIATES PLAY

Ⓖ   THE GOALKEEPER

☐   A DEFENSE PLAYER

1   A SPECIFIC DEFENSE PLAYER

4·   A DEFENSE PLAYER WITH THE BALL WHO INITIATES PLAY

G   THE GOALKEEPER

• • • • ·〉   THE PATH OF THE BALL ON A PASS

1, 2, 3   THE ORDER OF THE PASSES (WHEN MORE THAN ONE)

———⟶   PATH OF A PLAYER

– – – ⟶   THE PATH OF A PLAYER AFTER HE HAS THROWN THE BALL

——◁   AN INTERCEPTION

∿∿∿   THE PATH OF A ROLLING BALL

LACROSSE

1

THE GAME OF LACROSSE

Lacrosse is an Indian game and was used by them not only for recreation but also as a training school in which to quicken and strengthen the body. Its origin, however, is lost in the obscurity that surrounds the early history of this people. It was a sport well suited to the nature and development of the young Indian warriors and was very popular among them.

The original game had no fixed or definite rules, since each tribe laid down laws of its own. It was midway between a sport and a deadly combat, and often the players suffered death, loss of limb, or other serious injury. It was instituted as a game of pure amusement, and yet it served the purpose of accustoming the young warrior to close combat. The warriors looked for, and longed for, the grand anniversaries when hundreds would return from the chase and the warpath to attend the lacrosse tournaments. The descriptions of the game given by different travelers vary, but all were most enthusiastic and impressed by its wild beauty and originality. Two teams were selected to oppose each other. A ball was placed in a neutral spot, and the purpose of the game was for each team to obtain possession of the ball and, holding it in a pocket carved out of a stick, carry it across a specified goal line.

The earliest players used a stick about three feet in length, with one end bent into an oblong or round loop large enough to hold the ball.

The primitive Indian players usually appeared naked except for a tight breech cloth and moccasins. On grand occasions, they painted their faces and bodies.

Sometimes great matches were played between two tribes, and often entire villages were pitted against each other. The players were selected months in advance, and two weeks before the match the competitors began to train for the contest and to harden themselves in every possible way. The night before the contest, the players assembled on the shores of a lake and danced. This ritual served as a prayer for victory to the Great Spirit. Four of the medicine men who were to act as umpires sat praying to the Great Spirit and smoking their pipes. They prayed for impartiality in judgment and attempted to foretell the outcome of the contest.

At the start of the contest—usually at about nine o'clock in the morning—Indian maidens often ran forward and bedecked the players with beads and other tokens of affection. The two teams came forward to the middle of the field, waving their sticks and shouting defiance at each other. The old chiefs kept score. The most common way of starting the game was to throw the ball high in the air; the players scrambled for it as it fell to the ground. Sometimes the ball was placed on the ground, and at a given signal all the players would rush for it. It was never permissible to pick up or catch the ball with the hand, but it was customary to use the hand to bat it or to knock it down. Some tribes had a rule that to miss a catch meant the loss of the game. In some contests, the players used two sticks, one in each hand.

The original game was a wild affair. Sometimes as many as 600 to 1,000 players participated. They tripped and threw each other, and many players suffered cuts and broken bones. When two different tribes played, it was not unusual for several to be killed. Often two players engaged in a fist fight while the rest of the game went on. If the ball fell among the spectators, the players leaped into them, with little regard for their safety, but no one ever seemed to hold malice toward anyone else after the game was over.

There are some dark chapters in the historical record of lacrosse. In 1763, four months after the signing in Paris of a treaty of peace between the sovereigns of England, France, and Spain, an exhibition lacrosse game was to be played for the British garrison at Fort Michillimackinac. During the contest, the Indian lacrosse players suddenly turned on the fort and massacred nearly every inhabitant. In fairness to the Indians, however, it must be said that the British brought it on themselves. The French had been kind to the Indians and treated them as equals. When the British took command, the situation changed. The Indians were snubbed and abused. English fur traders cheated them, and settlers invaded their best lands and cut down their forests. Several plots to destroy the English garrisons between 1761 and 1762 were frustrated. Then came the "conspiracy of Pontiac." Pontiac was the great high chief of the Ottawas, whom eighteen nations had chosen as leader. He was a genuine savage, a born leader, with a courage that was contagious. Early in 1763, Pontiac had invited the Ojibwas of Michillimackinac to join him in the conspiracy, and they eagerly accepted. The English at the fort—thirty-five soldiers and nine other inhabitants —heard of the conspiracy but would not heed the warnings. The Indians were given unusual freedom and strolled about as they pleased during the daytime. June 4, 1763, was the birthday of King George, and the Ojibwas invited the occupants of the fort to witness a game of "baggataway," as lacrosse was then called. The Sacs were the opponents of the Ojibwas and the game was played on the plain in front of the fort. The gates were opened wide, and soldiers were lying or standing about in groups. The players, nearly naked, started to play. They yelled and screamed, chased and fought for the ball, tumbled over each other, kicked and wrestled with might and main. Suddenly the ball soared into the air and fell near the pickets of the fort. The players made a dash for the gates, and the warriors who were spectators followed them. The war whoop rang out, and the soldiers and traders were cut down without mercy. Not a Frenchman was touched, and about twenty men escaped death.

As early as 1839, the Montreal Lacrosse Club was formed and played several matches with the Indians. The game first gained popularity in Montreal about 1856 when Iroquois Indians of Caughnawaga introduced it as a field sport. In 1861, a game of lacrosse was played before His Royal Highness, The Prince of Wales, between the Canadians and the Indians. Twenty-five players participated on each team, and the game ended in a dispute when the Indian captain held the ball in his hand just as the whites seemed to have an opportunity to score. The match was awarded to the Canadians. After this, interest in the game ebbed in Montreal, but it revived in Ottawa.

In June, 1867, the Montreal Club formulated the first rules of lacrosse, and in September of the same year a convention ws held for all interested in the sport. This convention organized the National Lacrosse Association of Canada, amended the rules of the game, and adopted a constitution.

Also in 1867, a club was organized in Glasgow, Scotland. In July of that year, eighteen Caughnawaga Indians went to England and France and played several exhibition games. This was the origin of the sport in England.

The Mohawk Club of Troy, New York, pioneered the game in the United States in 1868.

As the white man became more and more enthusiastic about the game, he changed the general procedure, while at the same time retaining its outstanding features. Only savages could and would play the original game and accept the injuries that resulted with such stoic indifference. Rules were devised to prohibit tripping, fighting, pushing, holding, unnecessary slashing with the stick, and touching the ball with the hand. The size of the playing field was restricted, and the purpose of the game was for one team to throw the ball into a goal defended by the other team. The number of players on a team was restricted to twelve. The players assigned to defend the goal were given the following titles: goalkeeper, point, cover-point, second defense, third defense, and first defense; the attacking players were called center, third attack, second attack, first attack, out-home, and in-home. In 1933, the number of players on a team was reduced to ten, and it is the same today. The titles, however, have been simplified to attack players, midfield players, defense players, and goalkeeper.

In the early days of the sport, the players wore as little clothing as possible. Today, players wear helmets, face masks, cleated shoes, gloves, and thick-padded jerseys or arm pads and shoulder pads. The present method of starting a game originated soon after the introduction of the present stick form. The old method—throwing the ball in the air—did not permit an opportunity for skill. The current method requires knack and art, which is obvious to any who have witnessed well-drilled lacrosse teams.

THE FIELD AND THE GOALS

Lacrosse is played on a *field* 110 yards long and 60 yards wide. The goals are 80 yards apart, with 15 yards of playing territory behind each goal.

Each *goal* consists of two poles 6 feet apart, extending 6 feet out of the ground, and joined by a rigid top cross-bar. The poles (about 2 inches in diameter) are fitted with a pyramid-shaped cord netting of not more than 1½ inches mesh. Although 2-inch pipe is the best, many teams use 1-inch pipe, and some use wooden posts. The netting is fastened to a stake in the ground at a point 7 feet in back of the center of the goal. The netting must be fastened close to the ground to prevent the ball from passing through it.

A circle around the goal is known as the *goal crease*. This circle has a radius of 9 feet and should be clearly marked by a white line. The center of the circle is midway between the goal posts (see Diagram 1).

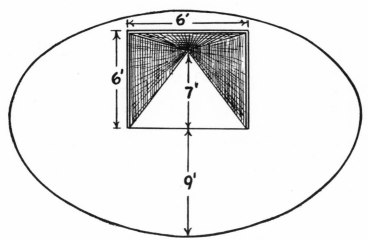

DIAGRAM 1.   THE GOAL AND CREASE.

The boundary lines are composed of two *side lines* and two *end lines*. These are marked out in white, as is a *center line*, drawn across the middle of the field perpendicular to the side lines. The field must have a white line, parallel to the center line, 20 yards directly in front of each goal. The territory extending from these lines to the end lines is called the *goal area*. Also there must be a white line 20 yards long on each side of the field and parallel to the side lines. These lines extend 10 yards on either side of the center line. The territory between these lines and the side lines is called the *wing area* (see Diagram 2).

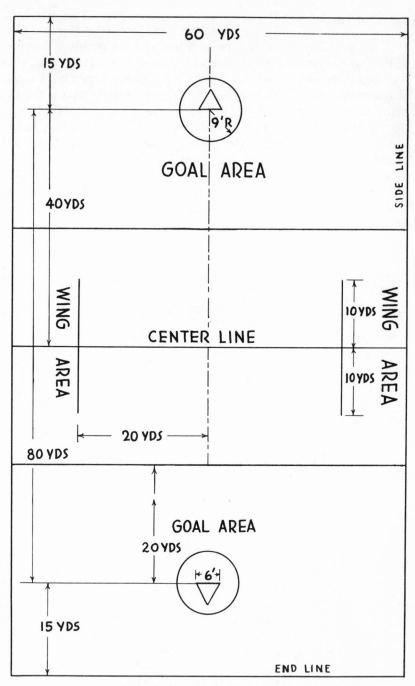

DIAGRAM 2.   THE FIELD OF PLAY.

8

THE PLAYERS

Ten players compose a team. Although the original names of the players are retained for historic reasons, it has been found less confusing to call the three players who play closest to their own goal the defense men; the players who play both attack and defense the midfield players, one of whom is the center; and the three men who play closest to their opponents' goal the attack players. The tenth man is, of course, the goalkeeper, or "goalie." Sometimes the words "close defense" or "close attack" are used to distinguish these men from the midfielders. The point, cover-point, and first defense are the defense men; the second defense, center, and second attack are the midfielders; and the first attack, out-home, and in-home are the attack men.

Before each game, the players on the two opposing teams line up at the center of the field, facing each other with their left sides toward the goal they are defending. Originally, the reason for this lineup was to enable the officials to inspect the players' equipment, since in the early days there was considerable use of illegal sticks and illegal shoes. Now, the purpose of this lineup is to allow the players to meet their opponents. This method of lining up for each contest is unique to lacrosse and extremely colorful.

	TEAM A		TEAM B	
	GOALKEEPER	IN-HOME		
DEFENSE	POINT	OUT-HOME	ATTACK	
	COVER-POINT	FIRST ATTACK		
	FIRST DEFENSE	SECOND ATTACK		
MIDFIELD	SECOND DEFENSE	CENTER	MIDFIELD	
	CENTER	SECOND DEFENSE		
	SECOND ATTACK	FIRST DEFENSE		
ATTACK	FIRST ATTACK	COVER-POINT	DEFENSE	
	OUT-HOME	POINT		
	IN-HOME	GOALKEEPER		

To start the game and after a goal has been scored, the teams line up as indicated in Diagram 3. Circles indicate players on Team A; squares, Team B.

Before play starts at the center of the field, the players are confined to the following positions on the field: the center at the center of the field; one midfielder in one wing area and the remaining midfielder in the other; the attack in the attack goal area; and the goalie

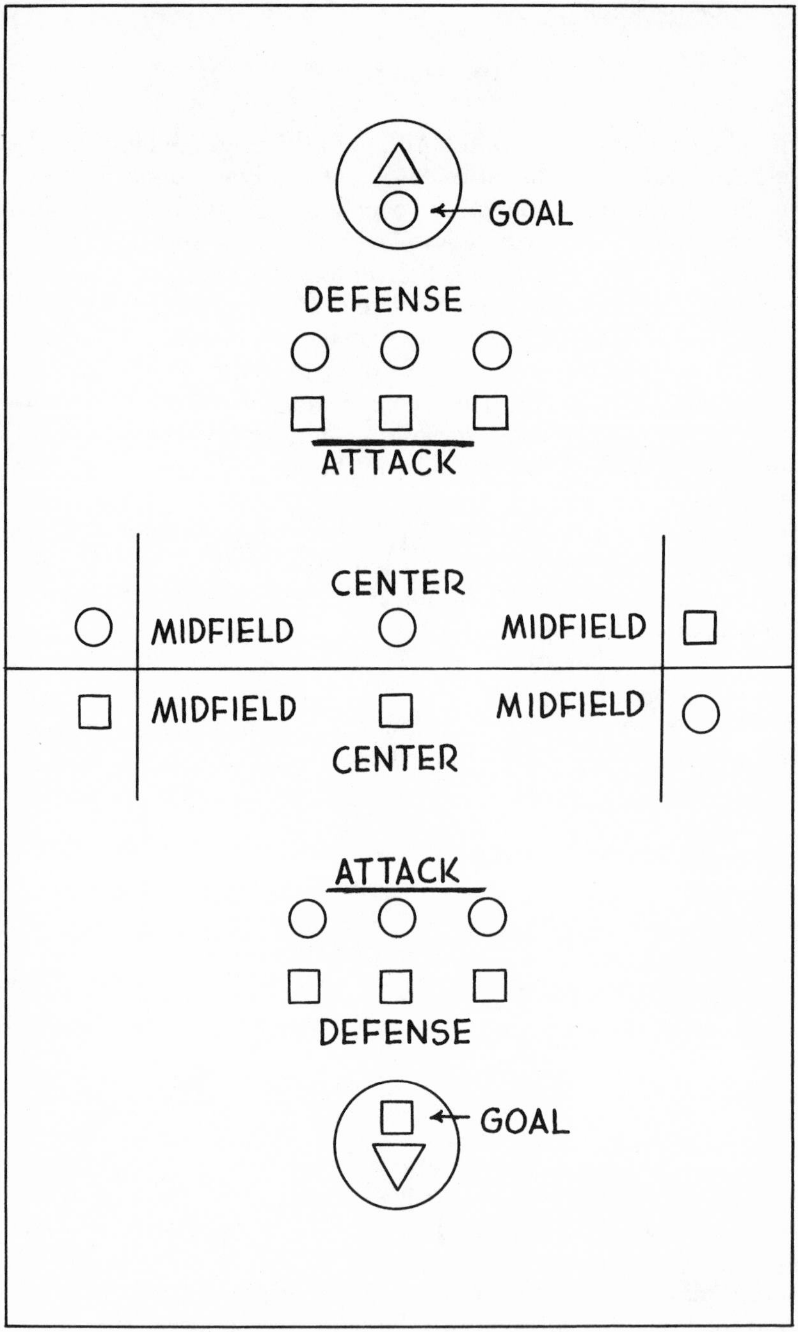

DIAGRAM 3. THE LINEUP.

and defense in the defense goal area. So long as the proper numbers of players are in the assigned areas, it does not matter what
position any one man plays throughout the game. For example, at
the face-off, a close-attack man could face the ball and the center
could play in the attack goal area. In case a penalty has deprived
a team of one or more players, that team is exempt from confining
its players to the wing and attack goal areas to the extent of the number of players in the penalty box. It also has a right to choose in
which area it shall exercise its exemption.

As soon as the whistle blows, starting the game, the midfielders
are released from their positions in the wing area. The attack and
defense players remain confined to the goal areas until one of the
midfield players has gained possession of the ball or the loose ball
crosses one of the goal area lines. When either of these things
happens, all players are allowed the freedom of the field within its
boundaries, with one exception: Three attack men and four defense
men must always remain on their respective sides of the center line.

THE EQUIPMENT

Besides a marked field on which to play and a pair of goals, it
is necessary to have a ball, and each player must have a stick, a
helmet, gloves, and a uniform. It is illegal for any player to participate in any of the play without a stick in his hand.

The Ball

The ball is of rubber, between 7¾ and 8 inches in circumference
and between 5 and 5¼ ounces in weight. When dropped from a
height of 72 inches upon a hardwood floor, it should have a bounce
of not less than 45 inches and not more than 49 inches.

The Stick

The stick is known as a "crosse," from which the game derives its
name. Sticks are either right- or left-handed, although today almost everyone plays with a right-handed stick.

The stick is made up of the *handle* and the *head* (*net* or *face*)
joined together at the *throat* (see Diagram 4). The net is bound on
either side by a *wall*. One wall shall be made of wood and the
other of cat-gut. For a right-handed stick, the right wall is always
wooden; for a left-handed stick, the left wall is always wooden.
The net may be made of leather, clock-cord, cat-gut, or nylon.

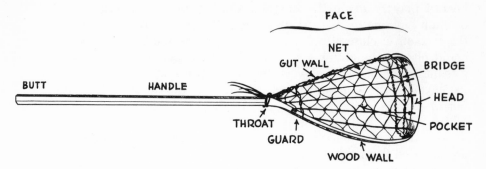

DIAGRAM 4.   THE STICK.

The *guard* is a mat of leather or rawhide that prevents the ball from being held fast in the narrow part of the net. There must be no peculiar fastening to the net that might make it difficult for the ball to be dislodged by an opponent.

The *pocket* is the portion of the net that holds the ball. It is adjustable. Each player should develop, or "break in," the pocket of his own stick. To keep the wall straight and stiff, the strings forming the pocket and the wall should be loosened after each practice or game and then tightened before the next one begins. In wet weather, the player should oil the net strings slightly, to keep them from becoming taut and lifeless, but never the wall.

The width of the stick cannot be more than 12 inches or less than 7 inches, and the length cannot be more than 72 inches or less than 40 inches. The length of the stick varies with the individual player's ability to handle it efficiently. Four face sizes are commonly used by most teams; a small face for the close attack (7 to 8 inches), a medium-size face for the midfield players (8 inches), a larger face for the close defense (10 inches), and a still larger face for the goalie (12 inches). The attacking player uses a stick with a small face to enable him to make short, snappy passes, to allow him to shoot quickly from any position, and to permit him to dodge without losing the ball. The close-defense player prefers a stick with a large net and a long handle to enable him to intercept passes, block shots, and prevent dodging. The midfield players are both attack and defense players, and hence their sticks must be medium in both the size of the net and the length of the handle. The goalkeeper uses a stick with the largest face of all in order to help him stop the ball from going into the goal.

The Helmet and Gloves

The lacrosse headgear is a strong light helmet with a visor, to protect the base of the player's head, his ears, and the outer corners of his eyebrows. The helmet has webbing in the crown to guard against hard blows (see Diagram 5). Gloves, either mitt or finger style, are of heavy leather to protect the hands. They are similar to ice-hockey gloves, notably in the heavy wrist guards. A mask to protect the face must be fastened to the helmet.

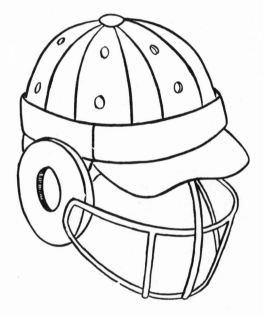

DIAGRAM 5.   THE HELMET.

The Uniform

The uniform of a lacrosse player consists of a long-sleeved jersey, shoulder and arm pads (unless the jersey is padded), shorts, socks, and shoes. The shoes should be of light pliable kangaroo leather, leather-cleated. Each player has a number marked clearly on his uniform, front and back. The goalkeeper should wear a metal supporter and some form of padding to cover the solar-plexus. The pad covering the solar-plexus need only be about 8 by 10 inches. It can be either fastened to the jersey or hung in place underneath the jersey by a cord around the neck. The shinbone, the most sensitive part of the leg, may be protected by small shin guards. The goalie should not wear anything bulky that will hinder his speed, impede his ability to receive and catch the ball, or prevent him from seeing clearly.

THE GAME

Lacrosse is played by two teams of ten players each, each team attacking the opponents' goal and defending its own. The object of both sides is to put the ball into the goal of the opponents and to prevent it from going into their own, and all the running, dodging, passing, and checking tend to that end. The ball may not be touched by the hands except by the goalkeeper when attempting to prevent the scoring of a goal. The ball is kept in play by being carried, thrown, or batted with the stick or kicked in any direction within the confines of the playing field.

A game is sixty minutes in length, divided into four quarters of fifteen minutes each. There is a two-minute interval between the first and second quarters and between the third and fourth quarters. Between the second and third quarters is an intermission of ten minutes during which the teams may leave the field. If at the end of the regular playing time the score is tied, play is resumed after an intermission of five minutes, for two five-minute periods. Whichever team scores the greatest number of goals in the two overtime periods is declared the winner. If the score is still tied at the end of these periods, the game is declared a tie.

At the beginning of each quarter and after each goal is scored, play is started in the center of the field by a draw, or face-off, between the two center players. The two centers put the *backs* of the nets of their sticks together at the center of the field so that the plane of the stick is perpendicular to the playing field and parallel to the center line. The centers allow their sticks to rest upon the ground and crouch facing the goals they are attacking. The referee places the ball between and touching the two nets and starts play by blowing a whistle. At the whistle, each center attempts to have his team get possession of the ball, either by controlling it himself or by passing it to a teammate.

A brief listing of the basic rules other than those previously discussed follows. For more detailed explanations of the rules, refer to the latest edition of the *Official NCAA Lacrosse Guide*.

1. No *attacking* player may enter the goal crease. The goalkeeper cannot re-enter the crease while carrying the ball. A defense

man cannot enter the crease while carrying the ball. In each of the above cases, stepping on the line is considered a violation of the rules.

2. Only the goalkeeper may touch the ball with his hand. He may, in protection of his goal, bat the ball with his hand or stop it with his crosse, hand, or body. He may not, however, catch or hold the ball in his hand.

3. If a player loses his crosse during the game, he is automatically out of the play until he recovers it.

4. If the ball crosses a boundary line (except on a shot), it is given at the spot where it went out of bounds as a free throw to the side opposite to the last player who touched it. If the ball crosses any boundary line as a consequence of a shot, regardless of how it may have been deflected, it is given as a free throw to the nearest player to it when it crosses the line. When the officials do not know who caused the ball to go out of bounds, the ball is faced 20 feet from the boundary.

5. When the ball is faced, the attacking player always faces his goal. The nets of the sticks are placed back to back, perpendicular to an imaginary line running from the ball to the nearest goal. The ball is never faced closer than 20 yards to the goal in any direction.

6. No unnecessary roughness or unsportsmanlike conduct is allowed. This includes fighting, hitting the body with the stick, tripping, body-checking from the rear, or any other illegal check.

7. No player may interfere with the progress of an opponent unless the opponent has possession of the ball, or unless both players are within 15 feet of a loose ball.

8. If a team has less than three attack players on the opponents' side of the field, or less than four defense players on its own side of the field, an off-side situation is called, and the team is penalized.

9. Each team is allowed to have a certain number of "time outs" during the game. (See *Official NCAA Lacrosse Guide* for further details.)

The penalties are either an exchange of the ball or the expulsion of a player from the game for a time to be decided on by the referee. Generally this time varies from thirty seconds to two minutes.

2

STICK TECHNIQUE

Lacrosse is a game of wits and not of brawn. If a boy is intelligent, if he is *a good stick handler,* and if he can run, there is a place for him on any lacrosse team. "A good stick handler" has been italicized because, regardless of the boy's intelligence or his speed, he is of no value as a lacrosse player until he can expertly catch and throw the ball. So, in learning to play the game, the novice must first learn the arts of handling and caring for his stick.

HOLDING THE STICK

To learn to grip the stick properly, the player should hold it horizontally, arms hanging naturally at his sides. A right-handed player grasps the extreme end of the handle with his left hand palm down; and his right hand, palm up, automatically takes hold of the handle at the proper place. A left-handed player reverses this procedure. Emphasize two things; first, one hand must be at the extreme end of the stick; second, the other hand is not necessarily at the throat of the stick (see Figure 1).

It is important that a player use as long a stick as he can handle skilfully, since a long handle gives him more reach both in catching

FIGURE 1. HOLDING
THE STICK.
A. Correct.

B. Incorrect.

C. Incorrect.

the ball and in preventing his opponent from catching the ball. Practice with sticks of varying lengths determines which length is the most satisfactory. Then, if the handle of the stick the player is to keep is too long, have it cut to the desired length.

THROWING THE BALL

The same arm and body movements are used in manipulating a stick to throw a lacrosse ball as are used in throwing a baseball. Many times it is necessary to throw the ball while on the run, but whenever possible the player should stop before making a pass. Better accuracy can be secured in this way. There are three important throws: the overarm throw, the sidearm throw, and the shovel throw.

Overarm Throw

The mechanism of the overarm throw for a right-handed player follows. He places the ball in the pocket of the stick; then he holds the stick horizontally with his left hand at the extreme end of the handle while his right hand takes its natural position. He draws his hand up and back in the manner of throwing a ball. His left hand is now automatically drawn to the right side of his body, not much above the original level, and fairly close to his body. This places the stick at an angle, with the net above and behind his right shoulder. He brings his right hand forward, and at the same time moves his left hand slightly downward and in a vertical circular motion back toward his body. He brings his body as well as his arms into the throw. His left foot comes forward with his right arm; his trunk bends slightly; and, as the ball leaves the stick, the motion carries through until his right arm is extended its entire length (see Figure 2). When he brings the stick forward, he directs the face of his stick toward that of the person who is to receive the ball. A left-handed player brings his left hand and right foot forward, and the stick comes down over his left shoulder as he throws the ball.

To learn the body movements, the novice stands with his left side toward the receiver, looking at the player who is to receive the pass. The coach gives him the ball and has him throw it, using the motions described above. His left foot is now already forward, and as he throws, the trunk of his body will automatically bend forward. For a left-handed player, the right foot is forward and the right side is toward the receiver.

Sidearm Throw

For the sidearm throw, the right hand comes forward from the side instead of down over the shoulder as in the overarm throw, and the left hand moves first away and then back to the body in a horizontal circular motion. The foot and body motions are the same as in the overarm throw. For a player using a long stick, this is a very effective method of passing. Figure 3 illustrates the sidearm throw about halfway completed. Notice that the ball is about to leave the stick.

Shovel Throw

The shovel pass is so named because of the peculiarity of its delivery. While carrying the ball and without changing the position of his hands on the stick, a right-handed player extends his stick directly forward, twists the face slightly to the right, and gives a sharp horizontal pull to the right with the right hand. The right leg is forward as the ball leaves the stick. A left-handed player puts his left foot forward, twists the face of his stick slightly to the left, and gives the stick a sharp horizontal pull to the left with his left hand. Extensive practice of this type of pass will prove valuable to the defense men when they are clearing the ball from the defensive end of the field to the attack players waiting at the other end. Figure 4 shows a left-handed player who has just completed a shovel pass.

CATCHING THE BALL

Lacrosse consists of nine individual contests—each attack man endeavoring to outwit his defense man, each defense player trying to prevent his opponent from catching and shooting the ball. Every player must be able to catch the ball and to pass it to a teammate, even when closely covered. In order to achieve this, a player should always be in motion when catching the ball. When the ball is being returned from defensive territory to offensive territory, the receiver must make the catch while he is running directly away from the passer; but generally a catch should be made as the receiver goes to meet the ball. To get out of reach of the opponent's stick, a quick start toward the ball is necessary.

To catch the ball, the stick is extended forward so that the entire face is in the path of the ball. As the ball reaches the net, the player permits the stick to give with the impetus of the ball, and follows

FIGURE 2. THE FINISH OF THE OVERARM THROW (right-handed player).

FIGURE 3. THE SIDE ARM THROW HALFWAY COMPLETED (right-handed player).

with a slight twisting of both wrists. When a right-handed player is catching a ball on his right side above the shoulders, he twists the face inward; if the ball is between the shoulders and the knees, he twists upward; and, if the ball is below the knees, he twists outward. A left-handed player twists the face of his stick in the same manner when the ball is on his left side. In every case, the player always steps forward to meet the ball.

When the ball comes toward the head of the receiver, the face of the stick should be in the path of the ball. At the same time, the head and shoulders drop sharply to the left for a right-handed player, or to the right for a left-handed player. Again, the stick should give with the ball, and, as contact is made, the face twists inward.

When the ball approaches a right-handed receiver on his left side, he brings the face of the stick into the path of the ball by moving his right hand in a horizontal circular motion to his left side, his left hand acting as a pivot. As the stick gives with the ball, he pivots on his left foot and allows his body to make a complete turn while moving in a small circle. Then the stick is in position for an immediate pass and the ball is protected by his body. In Figure 5 A, a right-handed player has just caught a ball thrown to his left side; in Figure 5 B, the player starts to pivot about on his left foot after making the catch. When a left-handed player catches a ball on his right side, he reverses these operations.

When a right-handed player must catch the ball close to the left side of his body, he brings the face of the stick into the path of the ball by moving his right hand in a horizontal circular motion, his left hand acting as a pivot. Then he pivots on his right foot, with his left leg moving around from behind his right leg. His body thus makes a complete turn. A left-handed player reverses the operations. It is not advisable to teach this technique until the player has passed the beginner's stage.

A defense player catching the ball while moving away from the passer puts the face of the stick in line with the ball, extends the stick ahead of his moving body, and gives a slight twist as contact is made with the ball. In Figure 6, a right-handed player is completing a catch of a ball thrown over his right shoulder as he moves away from the ball.

Unless the receiver is in a position to take a shot at the goal immediately after receiving the pass, he must protect the ball from his opponent by turning to keep his body between the ball and his opponent. After running to meet the ball and catching it, a right-

FIGURE 4. THE SHOVEL PASS—COMPLETED (left-handed player).

FIGURE 5. CATCHING THE BALL. A. Right-handed player catching to his left side.

B. Same player starting a pivot after making the catch.

FIGURE 6. COMPLETING A CATCH OVER THE RIGHT SHOULDER (right-handed player).

FIGURE 7. LOSS OF CONTROL OF STICK. A. White checks exposed end of Black's stick.

B. Black checks up under White's stick.

C. Black checks down on White's stick.

handed receiver continues running in a small semicircle to his left, coming to a stop as he once again faces the scene of action. A left-handed receiver moves in a semicircle to his right.

CRADLING THE BALL

Every player must learn to cradle the ball so that it remains in the pocket of the net as he runs. The hand that grips the end of the handle should be slightly lower than the other hand. (If the tilting is too great, the ball will roll from the pocket.) The player bends his arms at the elbows and moves the stick gently with a combined arm and wrist motion. The arm movement is an up-and-down motion, which comes from the natural movements of the body as the player runs. The wrist motion is a twisting movement and should be just enough to ensure that the ball remains in the pocket of the stick, as wild swaying will dislodge the ball. Only practice and experience will determine the proper cradling motion. A good player never looks to see if the ball is in his stick—he learns to sense it is there. This comes from a knowledge that he is carrying the stick correctly at all times.

A simple exercise to learn to keep the ball in the pocket is to place the ball in the pocket, bringing the stick rapidly forward as if to throw and at the same time twisting the stick through an angle of 180 degrees. The object is to make the twist quickly enough to prevent the ball from leaving the stick.

TWO HANDS ON THE STICK

One of the most difficult things to persuade a beginner to do is to keep two hands on his stick. Yet this simple act may determine whether a player will recover or lose a loose ball, receive or drop a pass, or prevent or not prevent an opponent from taking the ball away from him.

Often, after a player catches the ball, he begins to run, holding the stick with one hand, or he reaches out his stick with only one hand on the handle to scoop the ball off the ground. This is very bad technique. A player cannot possibly have control of the stick when he is holding it with one hand, since there are too many opportunities for his opponent to knock the ball out of the stick. Figure 7 illustrates two possibilities. In 7 A, Black has possession of the ball and is carrying the stick with one hand. White comes up from behind and checks the exposed end of Black's stick, causing him to lose the ball. If Black had had two hands on the stick, White could not have made this play, since the end of the stick would not have been exposed. In 7 B, White is carrying the stick in one hand and Black, coming from behind, checks under White's stick. If White had had two hands on his stick he might have been able to exert enough pressure on the handle of his stick to prevent Black's blow from dislodging the ball. In 7 C, White is attempting to scoop the ball off the ground with only one hand on his stick. Black checks down on White's stick, making it impossible for him to play the ball. In fact, White may even have his stick knocked from his hand if Black's check is hard enough. If White had kept two hands on his stick, he might have been able to force his way through Black's check and certainly would have been in no danger of losing his stick. Furthermore, when a player has only one hand on the handle of his stick, he is not prepared to make a pass to a teammate who may have found an opportunity to break away from his opponent. Hence a chance to score may be lost.

There are three instances when, for a matter of a few seconds, it is permissible to hold the stick with only one hand. First, during a dodge (see page 83) when the other arm is used to ward off an opponent's check. Second, when a defense player is attempting to carry the ball to his attack and finds himself surrounded by attacking players—the defense man should grasp his stick at the end of the handle, carrying it close to the ground, and weave his way out of his difficulty. Third, when an attack man is attempting to get the ball away from a defense player. He may find it simpler to check hard on his opponent's stick if he holds his stick in one hand at the end of the handle, since in this way he has more reach and can get more power in his swing. Except for these instances, keep two hands on the stick.

SCOOPING THE BALL

Many times the ball is loose on the ground. In order to pick the ball off the ground, the player grasps the stick firmly in both hands, bends his body forward, and at the same time bends his knees. Now holding the stick nearly parallel to the ground, he shoves the top of it under the ball and scoops the ball up with a shovel-like motion. For a right-handed player, the right foot is forward and the end of the handle is outside of the left leg. It is important that the end of the handle be held away from the body to avoid jamming it into the body and causing serious injury. Figure 8 A illustrates the proper

FIGURE 8. SCOOPING THE BALL (right-handed player).
A. Proper position.

B. Improper position.

C. Proper position when ball is close to feet.

FIGURE 9. CHECKING.
A. White checks
down on Black's
stick.,

B. Black checks up
on White's stick.

position for scooping the ball for a right-handed player. Figure 8 B illustrates a player scooping the ball off the ground with only one hand on the stick. Notice how exposed the end of the handle is to a possible check by an opponent.

If a close-defenseman has to scoop the ball off the ground when it is lying directly at his feet, he slides both hands down the handle until the right hand (for a right-handed player) is at the throat of the stick. The two hands are kept apart at their original distance. Then, with knees bent and stick held at his side and nearly parallel to the ground, he scoops up the ball in a shovel-like motion (see Figure 8 C) and, as quickly as possible, moves his hands back to their normal position.

CHECKING

To check a player's stick is to give it a hard blow for the purpose of dislodging the ball or to keep a player from gaining possession of a loose ball. There are two times during a lacrosse game when a player is permitted to hit his opponent's stick with his own stick: when his opponent has the ball in his stick and when both players are within 15 feet of a loose ball.

An opponent's stick should be checked just as he is about to receive the ball, so that he will never have the ball in his stick. In Figure 9 A, White is about to check down on Black's stick just as Black has caught the ball. In Figure 9 B, White is attempting to play the loose ball and Black is checking White's stick upward in order to keep him from gaining possession of the ball and yet at the same time to give himself an opportunity to receive it.

Sometimes it is better to hit down on the stick and sometimes to hit up; individual circumstances are pointed out from time to time throughout the book.

EXERCISES (FOR THE COACH)

It is impossible to put too much emphasis on the importance of drill in fundamentals. Good stickwork is acquired only by hard, earnest, and sometimes monotonous practice. Spend the first two weeks of practice on drills patterned after the following exercises. After this, devote at least half an hour every day to fundamentals. Do not practice any one exercise too long, or it will become tiresome. Encourage the players to "talk" to each other during the drills.

Exercise 1

Formation. Five to ten players in a line with 10 yards between players. One of the end players has the ball (see Figure 10).
Objective. To pass properly, to run to meet the ball, to catch the ball, and to turn properly.
Procedure. Man with ball passes to the man nearest to him as he runs to meet the ball. As he catches it he turns, stops, and then passes to the next player, who is running toward him. Continue.
Suggestion. Stress accuracy in passing rather than speed. No player should start to move until the passer is ready to throw the ball.

Exercise 2

Formation. Players in line, 10 yards apart. One of the end players has the ball (see Figure 10).
Objective. To scoop properly, to run to meet the ball, and to turn properly.
Procedure. Throw the ball on the ground to nearest player. He scoops it up, turns, stops, and throws to the next player, who is running toward him.
Suggestions. Emphasize having the body in front of the ball as the scoop is made. This enables the player to stop the ball with his body in case it takes a bad hop. Be sure the stick is held properly. No player should start running until the passer is ready to throw the ball. Encourage the players to talk to each other as they play.

Exercise 3

Formation. Five to ten players in a circle at least 10 yards apart. One of the players has the ball (see Figure 11).
Objective. To make accurate passes, to turn properly, to scoop ball off ground, and to run to meet the ball.
Procedure. One player passes the ball to the next, sometimes in the air and sometimes on the ground. Continue.
Suggestions. Stress accuracy in passing rather than speed. Change the direction of the passes from time to time. Encourage talking.

Exercise 4

Formation. Ten to fifteen players in a row, one directly behind the other. Place the ball on the ground several feet in front of first player in the row (see Figure 12).
Objective. To keep two hands on the stick with one hand at the end of the handle, to hold the stick properly, to turn properly after scooping the ball off the ground, and to cradle properly.
Procedure. First player scoops up the ball, turns, stops, and passes the ball to the second player in the row. Place the ball on the ground again and repeat the exercise.
Variations.

Roll the ball *toward* each player as he comes forward to scoop it off the ground.

Roll the ball along a line perpendicular to the line of players as the players take their turns at scooping it off the ground.

Roll the ball away from the players as they come forward to scoop it off the ground.
Suggestions. Stress proper body movements and proper handling of the stick as the player scoops the ball off the ground.

Exercise 5

Preparation. Erect a concrete or wooden wall, 25 feet by 9 feet, at one corner of the practice area. Paint a goal, 6 feet by 6 feet, at the bottom center of the wall.
Formation. Players in a single file about 30 feet from the wall (see Figure 13).
Objective. To play the ball on a bounce, to back up teammates, to make accurate shots at the goal, and to improve stickwork.
Procedure. First player shoots at the goal and then goes to the end of the line. The second player recovers the ball, takes his shot, and then goes to the end of the line. Continue.
Suggestions. Do not let any player leave his position until the ball has hit the wall. Have players shoot for the upper corners of the goal. Have second player in the line back up the first player as he goes forward to scoop up the ball. Have players tell each other when they are backing up. Encourage talking.

Exercise 6

Formation. Ten to fifteen players in a row, one directly behind the other. One player, the passer, has the ball about 30 feet in front of the line to do the passing (see Figure 14).

FIGURE 10.   PASSING IN A LINE.

FIGURE 11.   PASSING IN A CIRCLE.

FIGURE 12.   ROW FORMATION FOR PRACTICE IN SCOOPING.

Objective. To make accurate passes, to go to meet the ball, to turn properly, and to stop before making return pass.

Procedure. The first man in line runs forward, receives a pass from the passer, turns, stops, and returns the ball to the passer. He takes his place at the end of the line and the second player continues the drill.

Suggestions. Alternate the passer frequently. Have the next player in line back up the man receiving the pass. Encourage talking.

Exercise 7

Formation. Twenty players in a row, lined up in pairs. The ball is on the ground about 10 feet in front of the line.

Objective. To develop teamwork, to learn to back up the play, to cradle, and to shovel pass.

Procedure. One player goes after the ball. His partner in line backs him up and, after his teammate has the ball cleanly in his stick, runs past him calling for a pass. The first player gives him a shovel pass as he goes by. Continue.

Variation. Have the players line up in rows, three abreast. Each set of three players takes its turn in running up and down the field passing the ball back and forth.

Suggestions. Have player backing up talk to his teammate, letting him know that he is there. Emphasize all types of passing, including the shovel pass.

Exercise 8

Formation. Twenty players in a row, two abreast. The ball is 10 feet in front of the line.

Objective. To concentrate on playing the ball, checking, and scooping.

Procedure. Players go after the ball in pairs, each man attempting to recover the ball for himself (see Figure 15).

Exercise 9

Formation. Players in lines, three abreast. The ball is on the ground about 10 yards in front of the lines.

Objective. To emphasize teamwork—one player attempts to keep the third player out of the play while his teammate scoops up the ball.

FIGURE 13.   LINE FORMATION FOR PRACTICE IN GOAL SHOOTING.

FIGURE 14.   ROW FORMATION FOR PRACTICE IN PASSING.

FIGURE 15.   PLAYERS IN LINES—TWO ABREAST.

FIGURE 16. PLAYERS IN LINES—THREE ABREAST.

Procedure. Two players, teammates, attempt to get the ball from the third player (see Figure 16).

Suggestions. Alternate the two who are playing together. Have the two playing together talk to each other. One must indicate that he is going to take the man so that his teammate can concentrate on the ball.

Exercise 10

Formation. Two rows of ten men each, facing each other about 10 yards apart. The first man of one row has the ball.

Objective. To stress accurate passing, proper cradling, going to meet the ball.

Procedure. Man with the ball passes to the player facing him in the other row, who goes to meet the ball. After each player receives the ball, he passes to the man facing him in the opposite row.

Variation. Throw the ball on the ground.

Suggestions. Men in rows do not start until the passer is ready to throw the ball.

SUMMARY

The purpose of this chapter has been to teach stick technique. In order to emphasize the important features, they are summarized here.

1. Throwing
   Grip the crosse properly. Go through the same motion as you would in throwing a ball. As the ball leaves the stick, be sure

the net is directed toward the person, or object, that is to receive the ball.

2. Catching

Put the entire face of the stick in the path of the ball, and let the stick give with a slight twist as the ball reaches it. As a general rule, go to meet the ball. After catching, always turn so that the body is between the ball and the opponent.

3. Cradling

The arms, bent at the elbows, move in a gentle up-and-down motion, while the wrists move in a gentle twisting motion. The purpose of cradling is to keep the ball in the pocket of the stick as the player runs.

4. Two Hands on the Stick

Whether catching a pass or scooping the ball off the ground, keep two hands on the stick.

5. Scooping

Bend forward, holding the stick nearly parallel to the ground, and scoop up the ball with a shovel motion. Bend the knees as well as the body. Be sure the hand is at the end of the handle and the stick at the side of the body.

3

THE FACE-OFF

The object of the game of lacrosse is to get the ball into the opposing team's goal. To do this, it is first necessary to have possession of the ball. Hence, the face-off, or draw, is an important part of the game. The team that can consistently gain possession of the ball at the face-off will have a decided advantage.

All of the players should know how to face the ball, since there are times during the game when any two opposing players may be called upon to draw. At the beginning of each quarter and after each goal is scored, the centers face at the middle of the field. Whenever a ball goes out of bounds after a shot and the referee is unable to tell who was the closest to it when the whistle blew, or who touched it last when it went out of bounds after a pass, the two players closest to the ball face for possession of it. If several players are scrapping for a loose ball and no one seems likely to gain possession of it quickly, the official may blow his whistle to stop play and face the ball in order to eliminate the possibility of injury.

TECHNIQUE

To execute the face-off, the center assumes a crouch position. He stands on the same side of the center line of the field as the goal he is defending, with his crosse resting on the ground along the cen-

FIGURE 17.   THE START FOR A FACE-OFF.

ter line. He must have both hands on the handle of his crosse and
not touching any of the strings; his feet should not touch the crosse,
and both gloved hands must be on the ground (see Figure 17). No
portion of either crosse may touch, the wooden walls must be ap-
proximately an inch apart, and the ball must never be touching the
ground. Both hands and both feet must be to the *left* of the throat
of the crosse. The hands must be at least 18 inches apart at the
beginning of the draw. The official places the ball between, in the
center, and resting on the wooden walls of the faces of the crosses.
When the official sounds his whistle to start play, each player may
attempt to direct the course of the ball by a movement of his crosse
in any manner he desires.

At every face-off, the hand closest to the throat of the stick
should be pressed tight against the ground. This gives the stick
more spring when the draw is made.

NORMAL DRAW

The most common draw might be called a "sweep" draw. To execute this, the hand near the throat is pushed forward in a counterclockwise motion as the whistle blows, while, at the same time, the end of the handle is drawn back sharply toward the body. The objective is to cause the ball to be forced out to the left, where it is then up to the wing man on that side to obtain possession of the ball.

FLIP DRAW

For the flip draw, move the stick forward and *upward* in a clockwise circular motion. The player who is quicker or stronger can force his opponent's stick back and flip the ball into the air, where he may be able to recover it and make a quick break toward the goal. Otherwise he may be able to direct the ball to a teammate. Figure 18 shows the completion of the flip draw. Here White has won the draw, the ball is in the air, and either he or a teammate should be able to gain possession of it.

If a player has a deep pocket * in his stick, he might try this technique on one of the facings: Instead of making a flip draw directly, he drops the stick with its back flat on the ground at the referee's whistle. If this occurs a fraction of a second before the start of a normal draw, his opponent's stick will pass over the one on the ground and the ball will fall into the back of the stick. He should immediately flip the ball into the air and start forward. Then, as before, he may be able to catch the ball or direct it to a teammate nearby.

REVERSE DRAW

If a center discovers that his opponent is stronger than he is on the draw, he should let the opponent proceed with his normal draw. But, at the same time, he should move his stick *back* in the same direction as his opponent's and try to direct the ball to one of his own teammates behind him.

* It is illegal, however, to have too deep a pocket in one's stick. See *Lacrosse Guide*.

Figure 18. THE COMPLETION OF A FLIP DRAW. (White has won the draw.)

CLAMP DRAW

Finally, if it is apparent that the opponent is both stronger and more clever in the execution of the draw, the best technique is to clamp the stick over the opponent's stick in a forward and downward motion as the whistle blows. At the same time block him with the shoulder. This shoulder block should knock him off his feet or, at least, put him temporarily off balance. Then, if the ball has rolled free, scoop it up and run with it or pass it to a nearby teammate.

THE CENTER

An ideal center is a tall, rangy player with lots of endurance. He must be able to make quick starts at top speed and be a clever stick handler. He should use a fairly long stick with a well-formed pocket and should know how to draw in different ways. There are many little tricks that can only be learned from experience. Often a center will find that some particular style of draw is especially suitable for him; this he can discover by practice and develop to perfection by hard work.

EXERCISE

Formation. Players line up in rows by pairs.
Objective. To become more efficient in drawing the ball.
Procedure. Give each pair a ball, and have them face.
Suggestions. Have the players alternate their partners so that defense, midfield, attack, and goalkeeper get practice in facing against each other.

4

FUNDAMENTALS
OF ATTACK PLAY

The attack is made up of the *close-attack* players and the *midfield* players. These are the men mainly responsible for scoring goals. Occasionally, a close-defense player will carry the ball down the field and attempt to score a goal. This chapter presents fundamentals important for any style of attack.

POSITIONS AND PLAY

Before an offense is begun, three key positions must usually be filled: one behind the goal, one on the crease, and one about 15 yards in front of the goal. Diagram 6 illustrates these positions. The numbers 1, 2, and 3 represent not three particular attack players but rather three positions that attack players should generally occupy when attacking an opponent's goal.

Position 1 is filled by different players as the game progresses, generally by a close-attack player. The main objectives of a player in this position are to pass and to back up shots. When not receiv-

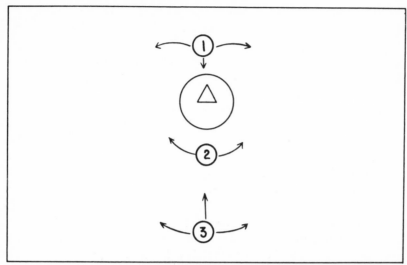

DIAGRAM 6.   KEY ATTACK POSITIONS.
Position 1—player behind the goal
Position 2—player on the crease
Position 3—player about 15 yards in front of the goal

ing or making passes, he plays close to the crease circle in order to recover loose balls and to be in position for a quick run around to the front of the goal for a shot. In general, he should cover the territory in back of, and about 10 yards to either side of, the goal. Any time a player in 1 leaves the position for any purpose, one of the other close-attack players must immediately fill the position. Most of the time *two* men are in back of the goal (one on each side), and hence position 1 is always occupied.

Position 2 is filled by any one of the attack players, but generally it is played by a close-attack man. It is an important position and a difficult one to play and requires diligent practice. The main objectives of a player in this position are to screen the goalkeeper from shots made by teammates and to be ready to recover a ball partially blocked by the goalkeeper and shoot it. This player must be an expert stick handler and be able to catch and shoot the ball almost simultaneously. If a midfield man plays here, he should not go behind the goal unless it is absolutely necessary. (Such a situation might arise if player in position 1, on recovering the ball in back of the goal, runs around to the front, takes a shot, and misses; if no one is backing up the shot, player in position 2 must play the ball and another player takes over position 2.)

Midfield players ordinarily cover position 3. The main objectives of a player in this position are to make quick breaks toward the goal in the hope of receiving a pass for a shot, to back up passes, and to take long shots. A player in 3 must always be ready to prevent an opponent from retrieving a loose ball rolling toward midfield and from carrying it down the field as an extra man on the attack. Note that, whereas position 2 is often covered by the same player during an entire game (or even every game), positions 1 and 3 are continually covered by different players as the game progresses. This situation occurs because, as a player in 3 cuts for the goal, one of the other midfielders moves into this position.

In order to give the attack room in which to work, a certain amount of territory must always be kept open in front of the goal. The remaining three attack players (4, 5, and 6) arrange themselves with 1 and 3 in a circle about the goal (see Diagram 7). Three men (3, 4, and 5) station themselves 10 yards apart and about 15 yards in front of the goal, while two men (1 and 6) play behind the goal. When 3 cuts to his right for a pass, 4 backs up the play and then shifts over to cover the position 3 previously held; if 3 cuts to his left, 5 backs up the play and then shifts over to cover the center spot where 3 had been. Players must not crowd one another or this territory in front of the goal. If the circle is maintained, individual,

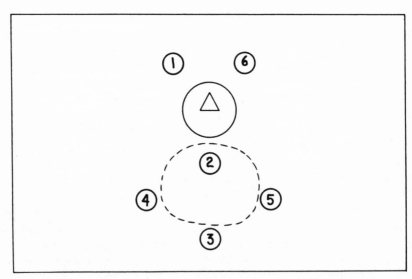

DIAGRAM 7. ATTACK PLAYERS IN CIRCLE FORMATION (dotted line indicates territory to be kept open).

systematic cutting for passes will follow, rather than haphazard, unorganized group cutting.

The attack must learn to keep its formation balanced in order to be in position to back one another up and to retrieve loose balls at all times. All players are eager to score goals. If they push closer and closer to the goal, the scoring territory, which should be kept open, becomes cluttered with players, and cutting and shooting become practically impossible. One reason for crowding is because midfield players play too close to the crease. They must learn that a player does not have to be on the crease to score a goal. Another reason for crowding is that the defense players sometimes drop back close to the goal to protect it, and the attack players automatically follow them. This the attack should not do. If the defense men play in close to the goal and fail to come out to cover their attack opponents, the attack players should pass the ball back and forth among themselves, working it closer and closer to the goal as they maintain their balanced formation. When some attack player is close enough, he should take a shot at the goal. Following a number of these tactics by the attack, the defense will have to come out to check or the attack will score goals at will.

The secret of keeping a balanced attacking formation is teamwork. Everyone must be alert and on the move at all times. Each player should participate in every play, even though he himself is not directly involved. For three or four of the attack players, this may mean merely a slight shifting of position—just enough motion to keep their opponents from interfering with the teammate cutting, passing, or dodging.

A little talk among teammates often helps prevent mistakes and helps the attack players keep the scoring area clear for offensive maneuvers. A player may be prevented from doing the wrong things if he and his teammates learn to talk to each other as various plays develop. Players can learn to do this during the drill exercises presented on pages 29 to 35.

TURNING FACING THE CREASE

When an attacking player recovers a loose ball or receives a pass and is not in a position to take a shot at the goal, he should always turn correctly (so that his body is between his opponent and the ball) and look for an open man in the scoring territory.

Many of the best opportunities for an attack man to cut by his opponent arise just after a loose ball has been recovered. The rea-

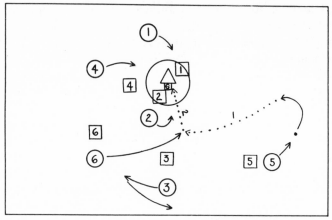

DIAGRAM 8.   TURNING AFTER RECOVERING A LOOSE BALL.   ⑤, a right-
handed player, picks up a loose ball on the right side of the field. He turns
in a small arc to his left to protect the ball and to look for a teammate to
whom to pass. ⑥ jumps by his defense man and runs toward scoring territory to receive the pass. ⑤ passes to ⑥ as ③ backs up the pass (runs to
a position in back of ⑥). ⑥ shoots at the goal. ① and ④ close in on the
goal to back up the shot and ② prepares to play a possible rebound shot.
③ returns to the middle position after ⑥ receives the pass.

son is obvious. When the attack has the ball, the defense is under a
certain nervous strain. After a shot is taken and missed, there is a
normal reaction of mental and physical rest on the part of the defense men. During this period of relaxation, an alert attack player
may find an opportunity to jump by his opponent and become an
extra man (see page 75). It is the duty of the man that has recovered the loose ball to look for, and be ready to pass the ball to, this
extra man. If a player in scoring territory has to call for the pass,
the effectiveness of the play is diminished, since the call will signal
the defense men to be on the alert. Each attack man must keep
mentally alert at all times, ready to recover any loose ball that may
be near him. (See Diagram 8.)

CUTTING

Each attack player has to attempt to elude his defense man at
some time during each contest. He gets away from his opponent by
dodging (see page 79) or by breaking away quickly (cutting).

Lacrosse is a game of fast breaks, and the entire play of offense is worked out with this in mind, but so often the plan is ruined by a lack of intelligent cutting. An attack player must consider two things before attempting a fast break. He must be sure, first, that his teammate, with the ball, is prepared for his break and, second, that there is a good possibility the play will succeed. Many times a player is free from his opponent but his teammate with the ball is not ready to pass the ball to him. The man preparing to make a quick break must be sure the passer is looking for him.

A player must never break if it is obvious to him that, if he does get free, his teammate with the ball cannot throw to him. Often the man with the ball is ready but cannot pass because of the formation. For example, if the attacking player has the ball on the right side of the goal, his teammate should not cut to the left side, because there is danger of the ball being intercepted by the defense. A player should never break if another teammate has already started to cut. Rather, he should keep the field balanced and get into position to back up the pass or the shot.

Intelligent cutting, because it minimizes the number of quick breaks attempted, conserves much of the energy and strength of the player.

SCREENING

The word "screen" is used in two senses in lacrosse. First, when the crease man places himself between the goalkeeper and the man with the ball, he screens the goalkeeper from the ball. As has already been stated, this is one of the objectives of the crease man. Second, when attack player A places himself in such a position that teammate B in running past him will lose his defense man, A forms a screen for B.

This process of screening is a vital part of attack technique. The midfielders should all take their turns at screening for each other. Nearly all offensive plays (see page 89) are developed from this screening technique. Diagrams 9 and 10 illustrate the second interpretation of screening.

PASSING AND SHOOTING

The fascination of lacrosse lies in the cleverness with which the players handle their sticks, in the smoothness of their teamwork, and in the speed with which they execute their plays. The effectiveness

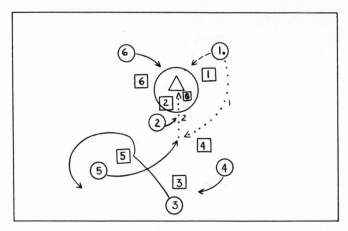

DIAGRAM 9. SCREENING. ③ screens for ⑤, who, breaking past ③, receives a pass from ① and takes a shot. After ⑤ goes by, ③ backs up the pass. ① and ⑥ go to the rear crease line, ④ backs up the middle and ② turns ready to play any loose ball.

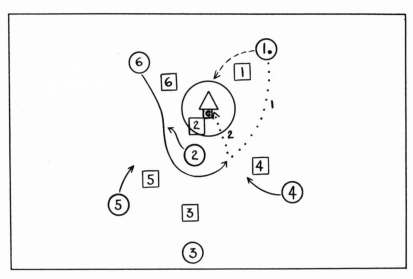

DIAGRAM 10. SCREENING. ② screens for ⑥, who comes around from behind the goal to take a pass from ①. ④ and ⑤ close in on their men. ③ backs up the middle and ① goes to the rear crease circle after he makes his pass.

of an attack is measured by its ability to bewilder the opposing defense. A diversified type of game prevents the defense player from watching his man and the ball at the same time, in a fast-passing, fast-moving attack. Keeping the ball constantly on the move, not just in a circle, but back and forth among the players, from back of the goal to the men in front, the men should take turns trying for an opening. Holding the ball too long gives the defense time to cover all players. It is not necessary for a shot to follow every pass.

A player should not pass to a teammate if he is obviously covered or if there appears to be danger of interception. A player can know when a teammate is obviously covered only through practicing and playing together, becoming familiar with his style of play. One player may not be open under a certain circumstance; while another player will be open under the same circumstance, since he may be more expert in his stickwork and may be able to catch a ball in such a position that the defense man will find it difficult to interfere. During the daily scrimmages, the attack players must learn to play as a unit, to study each other, and to think before attempting a cut, so that many wild, erratic, and wasteful passes will be eliminated.

For the most part, each player must decide for himself, at the particular time, whether he should or should not pass. In general, he must keep three things in mind:

1. A pass from in front of the goal to a player behind the goal is never used unless the attack player's opponent is far enough away to ensure non-interception. A smart defense man, by playing an attack player loosely, will attempt to cause a pass to be thrown that he can intercept. Often the goalkeeper can intercept passes thrown too low or too close to the side of the goal.

2. A pass to an attack player who is directly behind the goal gives him the ball in a strategic spot. However, if the defense is alert, it is not easy to accomplish this, because the goalie or the defense player can intercept these passes. Diagram 11 illustrates the territory in which it is permissible to pass to an attack player to the rear of the crease circle. If the defense man plays in back with the attack man, it is difficult to make the pass from any position.

3. The long pass *across* the field to a player who appears to be open is used sparingly because there are so many opportunities for the defense either to intercept the ball or to check the receiver as he is about to catch the ball. There is also danger of the ball going out of bounds and automatically becoming the property of the other team. Diagram 12 illustrates misuse of the long pass.

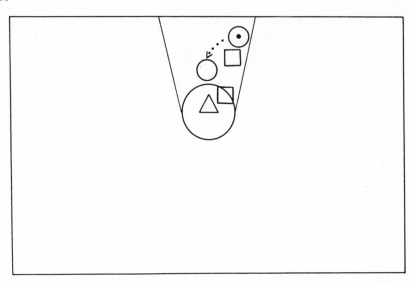

DIAGRAM 11. PASSING WITHIN PERMISSIBLE TERRITORY TO REAR OF CREASE.

To score goals, the attack must shoot, and shoot and shoot. The more shots taken, the more chances there are that some of the balls will end up in the goal. Shooting goals is an art. It is amazing how many times an empty goal can be missed! Hence it is essential that the attack men continually practice their shooting.

Some shots are more difficult than others for the goalie to stop. Probably the most difficult shot is one which comes over the shoulder—for a right-handed goalie, the one that is just over his left shoulder. Another is a ground ball to the right or left of his feet. A third is the shot that hits near the crease line and bounces high to the top corners of the net.

Long shots should always be made on the ground. They are more likely to score goals if they are well-screened by the crease man. A good time to take a long shot is when a crowd is milling around the crease or when a loose ball has just been recovered in front of the goal. Close shots should be made high and aimed toward the corners of the net.

It is during the scrimmages that the attack must learn to take plenty of shots. Shooting goals in practice is to an attack player what batting balls in practice is to a baseball player. As a rule, it is best to shoot on the ground. Whenever possible, some player should be in position to play a rebound ball following a shot for goal. Many

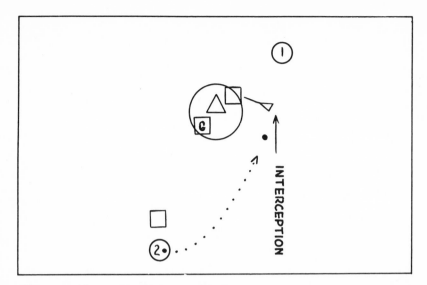

DIAGRAM 12. MISUSING THE LONG PASS.
A.   Attack player ② with the ball, playing in front of the goal, thinks that ①, playing to the right of and somewhat behind the goal, is open and throws him the ball. The pass is too long and ①'s defense man is able to intercept the ball.

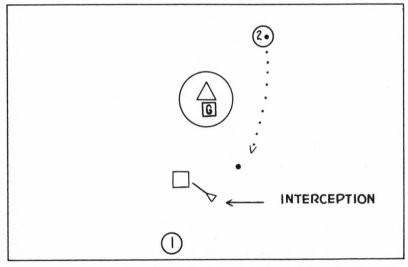

B.   ② has the ball to the right of and behind the goal. His teammate ① is to the left of and in front of the goal. The pass is again too long and the ball is intercepted. ② should never try this pass unless he is certain the ball cannot be intercepted.

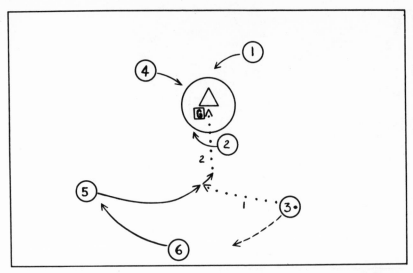

DIAGRAM 13. BACKING UP THE RECEIVER. ⑥ backs up ⑤, who receives the pass from ③. After ③ has thrown the ball, he moves over quickly to the center position. ① and ④ move in close to the crease line to back up the shot and ② screens the shot. All the players have a part in the procedure.

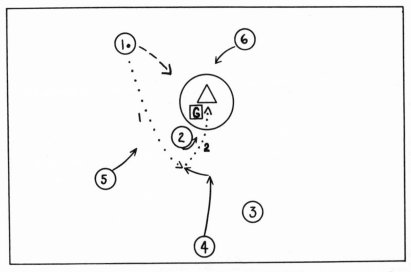

DIAGRAM 14. BACKING UP THE RECEIVER. ③ backs up a pass to ④, who shoots. After ① throws to ④, he runs to a position on the rear crease line. ⑥ also backs up behind the goal, ② screens the shot and ⑤ moves in closer to the goal, ready to recover any ball deflected near him.

times the ball is deflected off the goalie's stick into scoring territory
and an alert attack player can score on the rebound.

BACKING UP

Whenever possible, a player should back up a pass sent to his
teammate in order to be in a position to play the ball should his
teammate miss the pass or should his teammate's check interfere
with the play and the ball roll loose. All passes made to players in
scoring territory *must* be backed up, or many possibilities for scoring will be missed. For this reason it is extremely important for the
attack to keep a balanced formation. (See Diagrams 13 and 14.)

The midfield players must cover their men while shots and passes
are made by their teammates, to keep their men from intercepting
passes and from picking up loose balls that the attack players should
recover. Emphasize this because it is a difficult technique for the
attack to grasp. (See Diagram 15.)

The attack takes many shots for goal during a game; some are
wide of their mark, others are stopped by the goalie. Of the shots
that are stopped, some are not caught cleanly by the goalie but
rather are deflected back onto playing territory and become any-
body's ball. When the goalie does make a clean catch, his first
thought is to carry the ball away from the goal to a place where he
can pass to a teammate without danger of the ball's being intercepted or knocked into the goal. It is up to the attack men to take
advantage of every loose ball and to prevent the goalie from getting
the ball to his teammates. The attack accomplishes this by keeping
a man on the crease at all times, and by closing in (backing up) on
the goal as every shot is made. Of course, it is necessary to keep the
territory in front of the goal open, but the close attack should close
in on the sides and in back of the goal after an unsuccessful shot for
goal.

Backing up shots by closing in on the crease results in goals
being scored on rebound shots and in the ball's being in the hands
of the attack for longer intervals during the game. Also, backing up
may prevent the goalie from clearing after a save. Diagrams 16 to
18 illustrate backing-up maneuvers. In every case the close attack
should be as close to the crease as possible when a shot is made.
Most players have a tendency to stand still and watch the proceed-
ings after they make a pass or unless they are directly involved in
the play. This seems to be a difficult habit to overcome, and practice is required if one is to get over it.

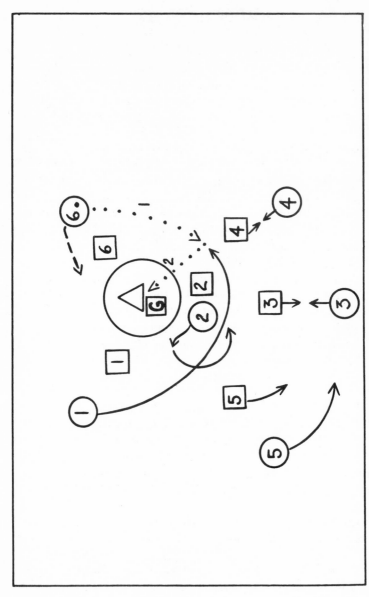

DIAGRAM 15. MIDFIELDERS COVERING THEIR OPPONENTS. ① cuts around from behind the goal to receive a pass from ⑥. ③ and ④ cover opponents to prevent them from interfering with the play. ⑤ backs up the pass and covers the center position. (If ③, ④, ⑤, play in close to the goal, ⑥ passes to ③, ④, or ⑤, who attempt a long shot at the goal.)

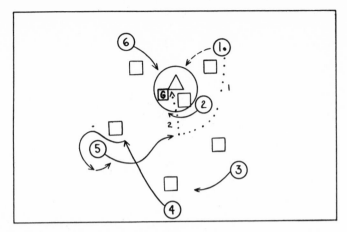

DIAGRAM 16. BACKING UP THE SHOT.

A.   ① has the ball behind the goal. ④ screens for ⑤, who cuts by for a pass and a shot. After ⑤ goes by, ④ backs up the pass and then moves in to the crease. ③ moves over into the center position and ⑥ backs up the shot. ② moves to the front of the goal, ready to play rebound shots. ① closes in on the goal after he makes his pass. After the shot, ⑤ continues on in to the crease. (If ⑤ does not receive a pass, he immediately circles out to the position ③ formerly held.)

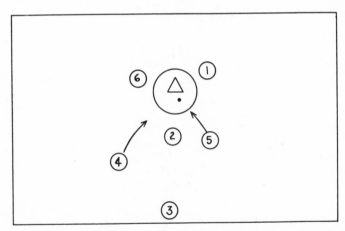

B.   Assume that ⑤ has taken a shot and that the goalie makes the stop and attempts to clear the ball. The diagram illustrates how the attack men can bottle up the goalie if they have placed themselves properly. ① and ⑥ take their positions on the rear of the crease circle, ② stays in front of the crease, and ④ and ⑤ close in on the crease circle on either side of ②.

55

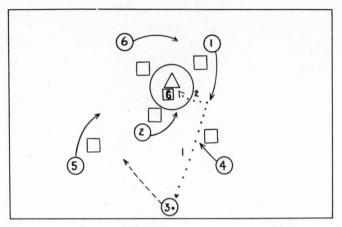

DIAGRAM 17. BACKING UP THE SHOT. ① cuts for a pass from ③ and takes a shot. ② is on the crease and ⑤ comes in toward the crease as ③ makes the pass. ⑥ backs up the pass and takes the place of ① on the rear crease line when he sees ① cutting for the pass. ③ and ④ merely move enough to keep the formation balanced. ① goes to the crease after his shot. (⑥ must be ready to recover the ball if ① misses the pass.)

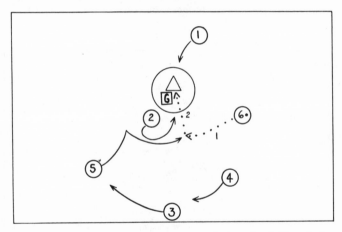

DIAGRAM 18. BACKING UP THE SHOT. ⑥ has the ball and throws to ⑤, who cuts for the pass and takes a shot. ③ shifts over to back up the pass, ④ covers the center zone, and ② is on the crease. ① backs up close to the crease line, ⑥ races to the crease as soon as he makes the pass. (⑤ must follow up his shot.)

CHECKING STICKS

There are times when it is more important for the attack man to keep his opponent from getting the ball (check the opponent's stick) than it is for him to make a play for the ball himself. For instance, when an attack player takes a long shot for the goal, his teammate on the crease screens the shot by standing in front of the goalie and, at the same time, attempts to lift his opponent's stick (check his stick) as the ball goes by. In this case it is better to *lift* the stick in order to prevent the possibility of the defense man using his stick to interfere with the path of the ball. Diagram 19 (page 60) illustrates another occasion when it is better to check the stick than to attempt to play the ball.

SUMMARY

The important fundamentals of attack play are summarized as follows:

1. Position

   Be sure to have men in the key positions about the goal: one behind the goal, one on the crease, and a third about 15 yards in front of the goal. Keep a certain amount of territory in front of the goal open to aid in scoring. Maintain a balanced formation to back up passes and shots.

2. Turning

   Turn correctly, facing the crease; that is, turn so that the body is between the opponent and the ball. Always look toward scoring territory after recovering a loose ball or receiving a pass.

3. Cutting

   Cut intelligently. Play as a team, and at all times keep alert to what your teammates are doing.

4. Screening

   Take turns at screening for each other as cuts are made for passes. Always screen the goalie as shots are taken.

5. Passing and Shooting

   Use short, snappy passes. Prevent the defense from getting set, by keeping the ball on the move. Do not throw the ball away or make a pass just because a teammate calls for the ball. Shoot at the goal at every opportunity.

6. Backing Up

   Back up passes. Every time a ball is missed, somebody has to get it. Be on your toes and in the right place, so the attack can keep possession of the ball. Back up shots. This means many more opportunities to score.

7. Checking Sticks

   Be alert for the time to play the man rather than the ball.

5

FUNDAMENTALS
OF DEFENSE PLAY

The defense consists of the *close-defense* players and the *midfield* players. The duty of these men is to prevent goals. Just as there are certain fundamental rules for attack play, so there are fundamental principles that each defense player should know and practice.

BALANCE

A defense man must cover his opponent cautiously and always be on the alert for a quick break, a dodge, a pass, or a screen play. He must be able to react quickly and to adjust his manner of play in order to prevent his opponent either from scoring or from assisting in the scoring. He must be careful to focus his attention upon the stick and body movements of his opponents and must not relax his vigil for an instant as long as his opponent has the ball. When covering the man with the ball, he should keep his body perfectly balanced on the balls of his feet—which means he must not cross his

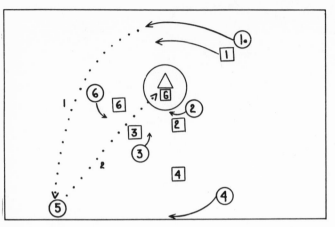

DIAGRAM 19. CHECKING THE DEFENSE PLAYERS' STICKS.

The attack has an extra man (⑤). ① carries the ball behind the goal from the right side to the left side and passes to ⑤. ⑤ calls "check" as ① passes. As the ball goes by, ⑥ and ③ check the sticks of the defense men nearest them to prevent them from intercepting the pass. ⑤ catches the ball and takes a shot at the goal.

DIAGRAM 20. PLAYING THE MAN. A. All defense players are in the proper position to watch both their opponents and ④, who has the ball. ⬚1⬚, ⬚3⬚, ⬚5⬚, ⬚6⬚ play their opponents loosely, since these men do not have possession of the ball. Since ④ has the ball, ⬚4⬚ plays him closely. ⬚2⬚ plays close to his man, since he is on the crease and in scoring position. If ④ dodges, ⬚3⬚ can easily pick him up and ⬚5⬚ and ⬚6⬚ can cover ③ and ⑤.

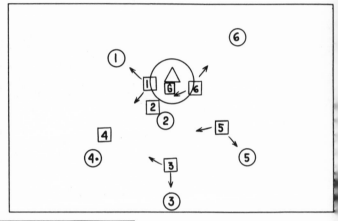

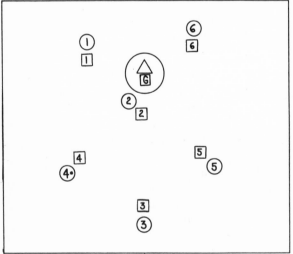

B. ⬚1⬚, ⬚3⬚, ⬚5⬚, ⬚6⬚ are playing incorrectly. They are too close to their opponents and, hence, if they attempt to keep track of the ball, the attack men have an excellent opportunity to cut by them into scoring territory. Secondly, they are not in position to pick up ④, if he should dodge past ⬚4⬚.

legs. Rather, he should sidestep as he follows the opponent, in order that he may change his direction practically as quickly as the attack man does.

To learn this sidestep, beginners form horizontal lines and take sidesteps, keeping on the balls of their feet as they take the steps. On the call of, "Right, left, right, left," the players change their directions. In order to keep them alert, the coach mixes the commands occasionally—"Left, *left*, right."

PLAYING THE MAN

A defense man should always remember that his first duty is to play his man, especially if his man has the ball. If a defense man's opponent does not have the ball, he must watch his man but he must also keep an eye on the man with the ball and his own teammates. He must play with split vision. If he finds it impossible to play his own man and watch the opponent with the ball, he should focus his attention upon his man. This is the case when his opponent has the ball, when his opponent is cutting for the goal without the ball, or when his opponent has placed himself on the rear of the crease circle without the ball. Diagrams 20 and 21 illustrate the right and wrong ways to play the man and watch the ball. Diagrams 22 and 23 show the defense playing properly.

Playing Between Man and Goal

To score goals, the attack must get in a line with the goal before taking any shots. To prevent the attack player from lining up with the goal, the defense man keeps his body between his opponent and the goal. Therefore, the attack player must dodge, run around, or pass the ball past his defense man.

There are two exceptions to the rule of the defense playing between the opponent and the goal. The first exception occurs when the ball is behind the goal. Then a defense man covering an attack player on the crease plays *behind* him and to the ball side. In this way he can see clearly what the passer intends to do and yet prevent his man from receiving a pass, by checking his stick as he attempts to catch the ball. However, if the crease man plays off the crease, the defense man should immediately get between him and the goal (see Diagram 24).

The second exception comes when an attack man is behind the goal and the ball carrier is in front of the goal. The defense man

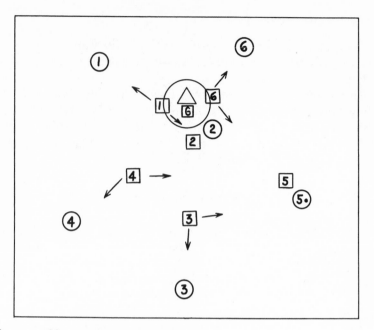

DIAGRAM 21. PLAYING THE MAN.
A (top) and B (bottom). In A, the defense players are in their correct
position; in B, [3], [4], [1], and [6] are playing incorrectly.

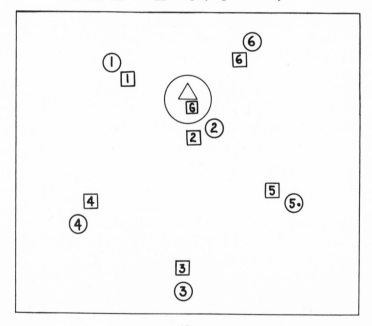

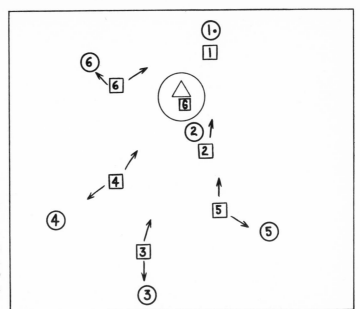

DIAGRAM 22. PLAY-
ING THE MAN. The
ball is behind the goal
and ③, ④, ⑤, ⑥
play their men loosely.
② covers ② closely
since he is on the
crease, but plays him
in such a way as to
watch the man with
the ball.

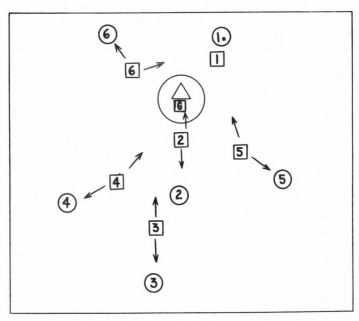

DIAGRAM 23. PLAYING THE MAN. The crease man ② is playing away
from the crease. ① has the ball behind the goal and ② places himself to
be able to watch the ball and his man.

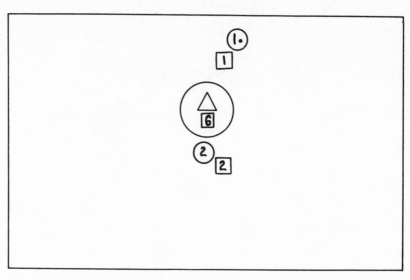

DIAGRAM 24. PLAYING THE MAN.

A.   The ball is behind the goal and ② is playing close to the crease circle. ② plays close to ②, a little behind him and on the ball side, ready to check his stick as he attempts to catch the ball.

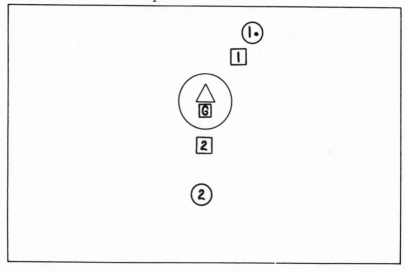

B.   ② plays off the crease and ② plays him loosely but between his man and the goal.

should not follow his attack man behind the goal until his opponent has received the ball or has been thrown a pass. If he remains in front he assumes the role of an extra defense man in case the ball carrier dodges. He also has many opportunities to intercept a bad pass or pick up a loose ball. He immediately picks up his opponent behind the goal when the latter is given a pass. (See Diagrams 25 and 26.)

Checking Sticks

To check, a player hits an opponent's stick with his stick. The purpose of the check is either to prevent an opponent from catching or picking up the ball or to knock it out of his stick (see page 29).

When an attack player is in *scoring* territory, he is a potential threat, and the defense man must give him undivided attention. Hence, when the ball is behind the goal, he cannot always watch the ball carrier, and the goalkeeper must keep the defense informed as to what is going on. In particular, when passes are made from behind the goal into scoring territory, the goalkeeper should call "check." At his call, the defense men in this territory check their opponents' stick whether they have seen the play or not. Many a goal has been saved by a clean, well-timed check that has prevented the receiver from catching the ball. This is not a foul as long as the ball is within 15 feet of the play. Figure 19 shows White checking his opponent's stick as the latter is about to catch the ball.

FIGURE 19. CHECKING THE RECEIVER. (White checks Black's stick as Black attempts to catch the ball.)

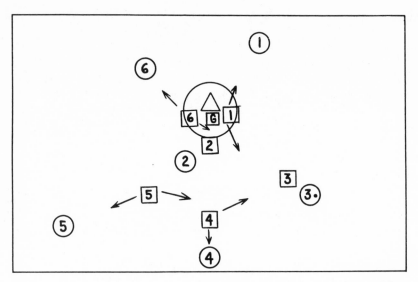

DIAGRAM 25. PLAYING THE MAN.   ③ has the ball and is covered by
③. ④ and ⑤ play their men loosely. Since ① and ⑥ are behind the goal
and the ball is in front of the goal, ① and ⑥ play on the crease in front
of the goal, ready to pick up ③ if he dodges or intercepts a bad pass. ②,
of course, covers ② closely.

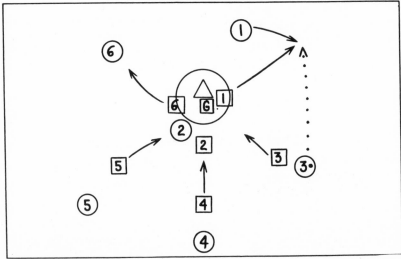

DIAGRAM 26. PLAYING THE MAN.   ③ passes the ball to ①. ① immediately covers ①, ⑥ goes back of the goal and plays ⑥ loosely, while ③
drops back three or four yards away from ③. ② still covers ② tightly, and
④ and ⑤ drop back toward the goal. ⑥ goes behind the goal to prevent
his man from receiving the ball directly behind the goal. This is a most
dangerous spot, since from there ⑥ could make short passes to teammates
in scoring territory.

Playing the Man on the Crease

To stop a long shot, the goalkeeper must be able to see it. There-fore, the defense man must prevent the attack crease man from screening the goalie and obstructing his vision. By checking the crease man's stick as the ball comes near and, at the same time, forc-ing him off the crease, he enables the goalkeeper to play the ball without interference. After the ball goes by, the defense man must not relax; he must be ready to cover his opponent's stick in order to prevent him from making a rebound shot. The defense man must remember, at all times, that he is not allowed to interfere with the free movements of his opponent unless he is within 15 feet of a loose ball or unless his opponent has the ball.

Dropping Back

As soon as the attack man makes a pass, the defense player im-mediately drops back 2 or 3 yards toward the goal. This prevents the attack from attempting a pass and cut play (see page 75). Dropping back enables the defense player always to be between his man and the goal. Now, even if the attack man cuts, the defense man, by his immediate reaction, is already in step with him and has a much better opportunity to prevent a successful completion of the play.

FORCING

An attack player carrying the ball is trying either to get close enough to the goal to shoot or to make a carefully planned pass that results in a shot. An aggressive defense player can prevent this by forcing his attack man to retreat and by worrying him with the stick so that he cannot make a good pass. Forcing the man with the ball means approaching him, closer and closer, causing him to drop back. To worry an opponent with the stick means to tap his stick as he holds the ball and also to hold one's own stick in line with the op-ponent's stick as he attempts to make a pass. The length of the defense stick permits the defense player to reach out and tap his opponent's stick. Often he can knock the ball to the ground, or at least make it difficult for the opponent to make a good pass. In Figure 20, Black is checking White's stick just as he prepares to make a pass. However, a defense player must be warned against forcing his opponent overzealously. A smart attack player who is a

Figure 20.   Checking the passer. (Black checks White's stick as the latter attempts to pass.)

good dodger permits his defense man to force him until he is enough in the open to attempt to go by. Every defense man must study the style of play of his opponent and cover him accordingly. He should play aggressively, yet cautiously, being careful to cover the shooting side of his opponent. If ever an attack man does dodge, it is the responsibility of the defense player to be sure that he goes by on the opposite side from his shooting side. This enables the man who picks him up to check him before he is able to take a shot. If the dodger is ambidextrous and can shoot from either side, the defense man must be very cautious in his forcing tactics.

BLOCKING PASSES

A defense man, with his long and wide-faced stick, should find many opportunities to block his opponent's passes, by keeping the face of his stick in line with the face of the attack player's stick. Then, as a pass is attempted, the faces of the two sticks come together, and the ball is knocked to the ground. In Figure 21 A, White has his stick raised preparatory to blocking Black's pass; in B, White is blocking Black's pass. Notice that the faces of the two sticks are together.

When a pass has been blocked, the defense man must immediately play the ball. There is no use in blocking a pass, if the defense man steps back and lets the attack player recover the ball.

A defense man must never relax as he attempts to block a pass; he should be prepared for a dodge and play the man aggressively, cautiously, and intelligently.

RUSHING

There are times when it is vitally important for a defense man to reach his opponent in the quickest possible time to prevent him from receiving a pass. As he runs toward his opponent, he must know exactly what he should do and how to do it. His intentions are primarily to knock his opponent off his feet—to rush him. First, his shoulder, with all the power of his body behind it, contacts the body of the attack man; second, he brings his stick down forcefully upon his opponent's stick in such a way as to block the pass or shot. Body contact is mentioned first because the attack man has an opportunity to sidestep the defense man and score if the defense man plays for the stick alone.

FIGURE 21. BLOCKING.
A. White prepares to block Black's pass.

B. White blocks Black's pass.

If an attack man is about to receive a pass and the defense man is sure that he can check him just before, or at, the exact instant that he is catching the ball, it is justifiable to rush him. If the man with the ball has dodged and another defense man is trying to pick him up, a rush may be imperative.

As a general rule, a defense player never rushes the man *with* the ball. An attack player finds it very easy to dodge when a defense man is rushing full tilt to meet him.

PLAYING THE LOOSE BALL

If ever a defense man feels that he has an even chance of getting possession of a loose ball, he should take that chance. This is a sound rule regardless of where the ball may be. In particular, whenever a defense player has succeeded in knocking the ball out of his opponent's stick, he should try to recover the loose ball.

Often, during the game, the ball is on the ground and several players are fighting for it. A defense man on the outside has a better opportunity of picking up the ball than any member of the scramble. With head down and eyes on the ball, he should charge directly into the crowd. As he charges, he calls, "Take the man," and, hearing this, his teammates endeavor to force their opponents out of the play. If it is impossible to get his stick on the ball, he should kick it into clear territory and take his chances of recovering it there. Sometimes he may be able to kick the ball directly to a teammate. If he can get his stick on the ball, he continues through and immediately breaks away from the group.

During a struggle for a loose ball, some players should remain on the outside of the melee and try to recover the ball when it comes near. Not more than two players on the same side should be actually involved in the struggle. The others should stand strategically close by and, by talking, help their teammate know in which direction to knock the ball.

Sometimes a defense player and his opponent are after a loose ball that is rolling away from them along the ground. If the defense man reaches out with his stick and pins the ball to the ground, at the same time stopping suddenly, he can often gain control of the ball while the attack man keeps on going for a few steps. Then, quickly scooping the ball off the ground, he can carry it to open territory.

SUMMARY

The important fundamentals of defense are summarized as follows:

1. Playing the Man
   Play so as to be able to see the ball, help out a teammate, and safely cover the opponent. If it is impossible to do all three, the most important is to play the man. Be sure to play between the man and the goal. Check the opponent's stick on *command* whenever in scoring territory. Never permit an attack man to screen the goalie on a long shot for goal. As soon as the attack man passes the ball, drop back a few steps toward the goal.
2. Forcing
   Worry the man with the ball, cautiously force him to drop back, and, if possible, knock the ball from his stick.
3. Blocking Passes
   Keep the stick in line with the opponent's, and make an effort to block any pass or shot.
4. Rushing
   Never rush the man with the ball unless it is absolutely necessary. If a rush is imperative, be sure to hit the body of the opponent with any legal body check, and at the same time attempt to check his stick.
5. Playing the Loose Ball
   Keep alert for every loose ball, and make a play for it anywhere on the field if there is an even chance to get it.

6

STRATEGY OF ATTACK

Lacrosse is a game of wits, in which the skill of the attack player is pitted against the skill of his defense man. In one way the advantage is with the attack player, since he knows what he intends to do, while the defense man must guess, and yet play in such a manner as to cause the least amount of damage if he guesses incorrectly. On the other hand, the defense man has an advantage in that he generally plays between his man and the goal. Although the attack man knows what he intends to do, the defense player has a 3- or 4-yard start on him before he goes into action.

Lacrosse offers each player opportunities to think for himself, particularly on the attack. At some time during every contest, each attack player has the opportunity to master a particular situation— whether to pass, to run, to dodge, to cut, to check, to try to intercept a pass, to go to the crease, or to take a long shot is a decision that the individual player must make on the spur of the moment.

After an attack player has learned what part he has to play as an individual, what he should expect of his teammates, and what they have a right to expect of him, he is ready to learn game technique. He must learn the different methods of attack: pass and cut plays, dodge plays, set plays. These are discussed in this chapter with other special features.

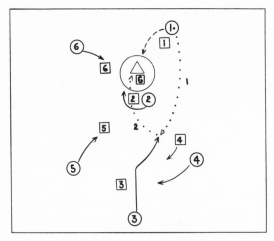

DIAGRAM 27. PASS AND CUT PLAY INITIATED BY PLAYER WITHOUT THE BALL. ① has the ball behind the goal. Suddenly ③ sees his opportunity and breaks away from his opponent. As he goes by his man, he receives a pass from ① and shoots for goal. (For this play ③ should be able to play right-handed.) Every player is involved in the play: ⑤ comes in toward the crease as the pass is made, and ⑥ closes in on the goal. ④ backs up the pass, ② screens the shot, and after ① has made the pass he moves quickly to the rear crease line.

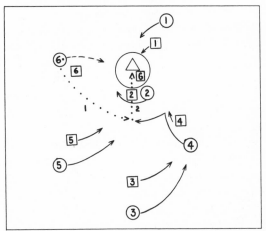

DIAGRAM 28. PASS AND CUT PLAY INITIATED BY PLAYER WITHOUT THE BALL. ⑥ has the ball. ④ breaks toward the crease, receives the pass and shoots. (A left-handed player has the best chance of making this play when the pass is made from the left side of the goal.) ⑥ closes in toward the crease after the pass, ③ backs up the pass, ⑤ cuts in toward the crease, ② screens the shot, and ① closes in on the rear crease circle.

PASS AND CUT PLAYS

The pass and cut play is the fundamental method of attack and is used continually during every contest. The play can develop in two different ways. In one, the player intending to make the fast break away from his opponent does not have the ball in his possession; in the other, he has the ball as the action starts.

Player Without the Ball

In this type of pass and cut play, the action must be natural and instantaneous. After the attack players have passed the ball among themselves for a few minutes, one of the players makes a sudden break to get away from his check. Sometimes he merely runs around his opponent, hoping to get loose by the suddenness of his actions and his speed; at other times he starts in one direction and then suddenly changes direction. If he gets open, he receives a pass from his teammate and takes a shot for the goal. If he does not get open, his teammates continue to pass the ball around until another player gets an opportunity to cut.

Passes made from behind the goal to the attack man are the simplest and best to use to score, since the attack man can receive and shoot the ball with the same motion and in full stride. However, breaks should be attempted from all possible positions: from the sides, from in front, or from directly behind the goal. Diagrams 27 to 31 illustrate several typical situations.

Player with the Ball

In this type of pass and cut, the man making the break has the ball before the action starts. The play is most effective against a defense that forces the man with the ball to keep moving away from the goal. When this happens the attack player should permit himself to be forced quite a distance from the goal. A teammate should keep within passing distance. Suddenly the player with the ball passes to his teammate and immediately cuts around his opponent. As he goes by, the teammate returns the ball to him and he carries it on in toward the goal. If he gets close enough, he takes a shot; if he is checked by a defense player, he makes a pass. The teammate who is to receive the first pass must place himself in such a position as to enable him to return the ball effectively and quickly. Diagrams 32 to 34 illustrate situations of pass and cut plays that the player with the ball initiates.

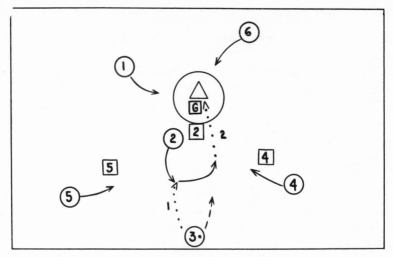

DIAGRAM 29. PASS AND CUT PLAY INITIATED BY PLAYER WITHOUT THE BALL. ③ has the ball. ② cuts away from his man directly toward ③ and receives the pass. He turns sharply and takes a shot at the goal. ① and ⑥ close in to the crease to back up both the pass and the shot. ⑤ and ④ come in far enough to attract the attention of their opponents in order to keep them from interfering with the play.

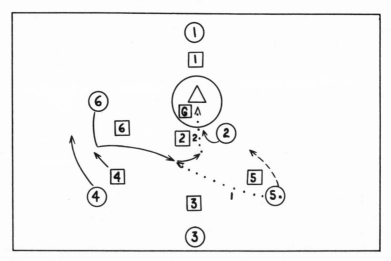

DIAGRAM 30. PASS AND CUT PLAY INITIATED BY PLAYER WITHOUT THE BALL. ⑤ has the ball. ⑥ breaks away from his opponent, receives a pass from ⑤, and takes a shot. ③ comes in and covers his man, ④ backs up the pass, ① closes in to the rear crease and ② prepares to play a possible rebound shot. ⑤ comes in toward the crease after he makes the pass.

76

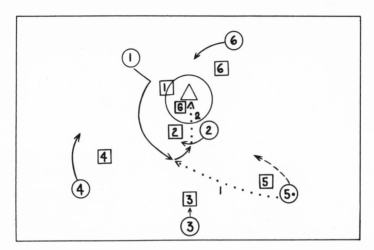

DIAGRAM 31. PASS AND CUT PLAY INITIATED BY PLAYER WITHOUT THE
BALL.   ⑤ has the ball. ① cuts by his man around the left side of the
goal, receives a pass from ⑤ and takes a shot. ⑥ replaces ①, ③ covers
his man, ④ backs up the pass, ② gets into position for a possible rebound
shot, and ⑤ comes in toward the crease after he makes the pass.

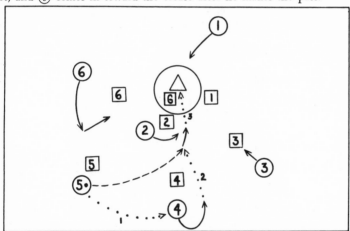

DIAGRAM 32. PASS AND CUT PLAY INITIATED BY BALL CARRIER.   ⑤ has the
ball and his opponent forces him away from the goal. Suddenly he passes to ④
and runs by his man. ④ makes a complete turn (if he is right-handed) and returns
the ball to ⑤, who carries it on toward the goal for a shot. ② screens, ⑥ backs
up the pass and then moves toward the crease, ① comes to the rear of the crease,
and ③ moves closer to the crease. (If, in a play of this type, ⑤ cannot shoot
because he is met by the defense man playing ②, he passes to ②, who takes the
shot. ② should be in a position to come to meet the pass, thereby preventing the
goalie from interfering with the pass.)

77

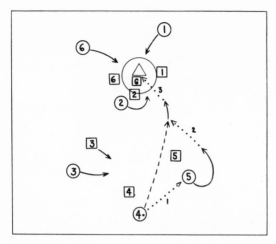

DIAGRAM 33. PASS AND CUT PLAY INITIATED BY BALL CARRIER. ④ has the ball and is being forced away from the goal by his opponent. He passes to ⑤, who comes to meet the pass, ④ breaks past his man. ⑤ makes a complete turn (if he is right-handed) and returns the ball to ④, who takes a shot. ② screens, ③ moves into the position that ④ held, ① and ⑥ come to the rear crease circle, ⑤ comes in to the crease after making the pass. The purpose ⑤ has in turning is to get him into position to pass quickly and accurately with the minimum possibility of interference from his opponent.

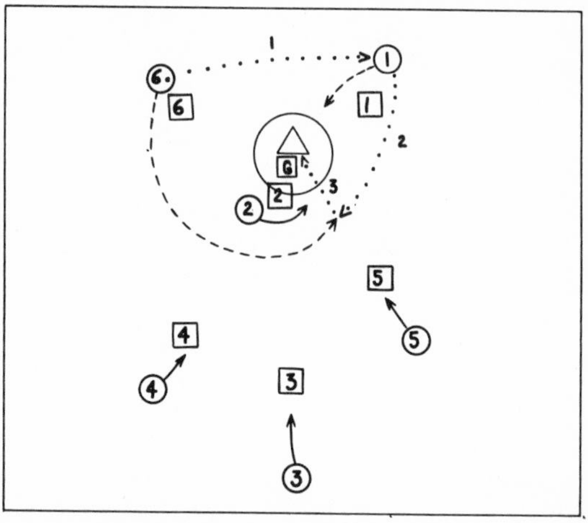

DIAGRAM 34. PASS AND CUT PLAY INITIATED BY BALL CARRIER. ⑥ has the ball behind the goal. He passes to ① and runs past his man around the crease circle. ① returns the pass as ⑥ crosses in front of the goal. ① runs to rear crease circle, ② prepares to play a rebound shot, ④ and ⑤ come in toward the crease, and ③ backs up the center position and the pass.

78

DODGING

Whenever a man with the ball is able to get past an opponent and still retain possession of the ball, he has dodged his man. The purpose of the dodge is to enable the attack to have an extra man for a few valuable seconds. Dodging is of tremendous value to an attack, but, if it is overdone, it retards the action and disrupts team play. Every player on the team should practice dodging, and every attack man should attempt to master at least one of the five types of dodge described in this book. Practicing dodging helps a player to develop poise, balance, footwork, and the ability to have complete control of the stick when it contains the ball. A dodger is a threat at all times and instils nervousness, tenseness, and uncertainty into the opposing team. He must be alert for a receiver after he dodges his man. Nine times out of ten a dodge does not result in an opening for a shot but rather in an opportunity for a pass.

The Running Dodge

The running dodge is the simplest for a beginner to learn and is executed by the player with the ball running past his defense man. Some players start this dodge by faking a pass and then suddenly darting at full speed past their opponent. Often it is necessary to stop suddenly and then start again several times before the defense man has been eluded. A player who can develop a quick change of pace should be very successful with this dodge. (See Diagrams 35 to 38.)

The Force Dodge

In the force dodge, the dodger, with his back close to his opponent, forces him toward the goal, protecting his own stick with his body and watching for an opportunity to go by. As he continues backward, he watches the legs of his defense man, because he can dodge best when his opponent's legs are crossed—when his opponent is off-balance. In order to set up this situation, the dodger should weave as he forces his way backward, pretending to break to the right and then to the left. If the defense player does not allow himself to be caught off-balance, the dodger must pick his own time for the complete break, being sure to go by his man on the side that permits him to make a natural pass or shot. (See Diagram 39.) There are two types of force dodge. One is slow and deliberate; the other

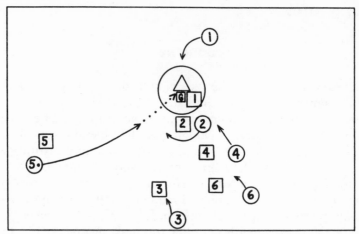

DIAGRAM 35. RUNNING DODGE.   (5), a right-handed player, draws far over to the left side of the goal and signals that he is going to dodge. (3), (4) and (6) move to the opposite side of the goal in order to give (5) plenty of room to go by. (2) plays on the crease away from (5), and (1) backs up in back of the goal. (5) fakes a pass, runs by his man, and takes a shot. (If (5) is left-handed he draws over to the right side of the goal.)

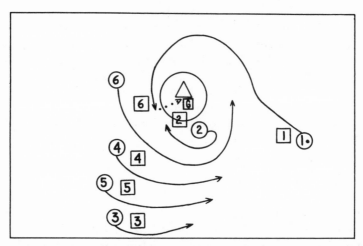

DIAGRAM 36. RUNNING DODGE.   (1), a right-handed player, signals that he is going to dodge and starts with the ball on the right side of the goal. (3), (4), (5), (6) gather on the left side of the goal while (2) plays on the crease. (1) runs by his man behind the goal and comes around the left corner to shoot. (2), (3), (4), (5) and (6) move to the right, drawing their men out of the play. (6) continues on around the goal to back up while (2) comes back to the crease ready to make a possible rebound play.

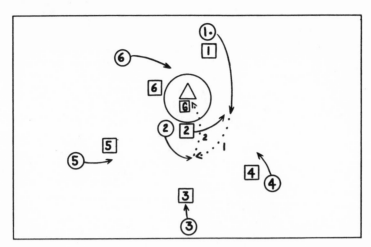

DIAGRAM 37. RUNNING DODGE. ① has the ball behind the goal and runs by his man around the right corner of the goal. ③, ④, ⑤ have drawn their men away from the play, ⑥ backs up the goal, and ② plays on the crease. Defense ② picks up ①. ② steps away from the goal, receives a pass from ① and takes a shot. (② must step away from the goal in order to keep the goalie from interfering with the play. If ① is right-handed, it will be necessary for him to make a shovel pass to ②.)

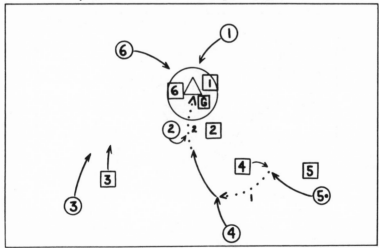

DIAGRAM 38. RUNNING DODGE. ⑤ dodges his man. Defense 4 picks him up and ⑤ passes to ④, who takes the shot. ③ backs up the pass and then moves in toward the crease. ① and ⑥ back up behind the goal and ② screens the shot.

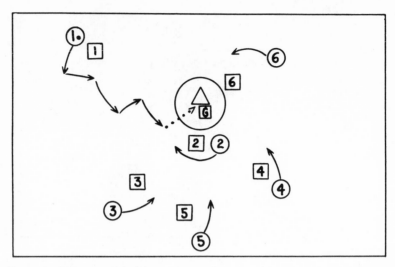

DIAGRAM 39.   FORCE DODGE.
A.   ①, a right-handed player with back to opponent, backs into his
opponent, forcing him to drop back. ① notices or senses the proper moment
to complete the dodge. ① then breaks fast around the left corner of the
goal and shoots. ⑥ backs up the goal and ② moves over to the right corner
of the crease. ③, ④ and ⑤ draw their men out of the play.

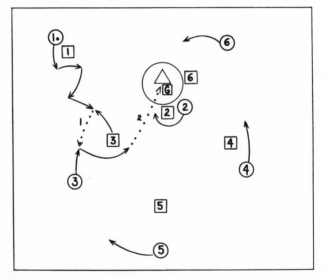

B.   ① is checked by ③ before he can get close enough to goal to shoot.
He passes to ③ who runs and takes a shot. (The play is most effective if
③ is left-handed.) ⑤ backs up the pass, ⑥ backs up behind the goal, ②
plays on the crease and ④ closes in to the goal.

is fast, with quick, sudden feints, first one way and then the other. The first type is better suited to the big man, while the other is more suited to the small quick player. Often it is necessary for the dodger to ward off his opponent's stick with his arm as he forces his way in toward the goal. This is only permissible, however, when the defense man attempts to check the attack man's stick.

The Dip Dodge

The dip, or face, dodge is difficult because it requires expert stick handling, good body co-ordination, and perfect timing. In making a dip dodge, a right-handed player raises his stick as though to pass. Then, as the defense man reaches forward in an attempt to check the dodger's stick, the dodger drops his head and shoulders quickly to the left; at the same time, evading the defense stick, he brings his stick forward, twisting it through an angle of 180 degrees in order to keep the ball in his stick. The right leg comes *forward,* crossing the left leg, and the dodger continues on past his defense man. For a left-handed player, the motions are reversed.

The Circle Dodge

The circle dodge is performed by the dodger going swiftly toward his opponent. As he reaches him, he wheels on his left foot through a complete revolution, throwing himself forward at the same time. As he spins, he holds the stick nearly vertical in order to keep the ball from falling out.

The Toss Dodge

As the dodger gets close to his opponent, he flips the ball around his opponent, runs by him, scoops the ball off the ground and continues on toward the goal. The dodger must be careful to direct the ball to a spot that he expects to reach quickly after he goes by. (See Diagram 40.)

Dodge Plays

The important and most difficult things for a player to learn are when to dodge and what to do after he dodges. He should never dodge when the field is crowded with players. The dodger should generally be 15 or more yards away from the goal and, whenever possible, should indicate his intentions of dodging to his teammates.

The signal for dodging can be given by (1) waving the players away with the hand or (2) calling out some prearranged number or

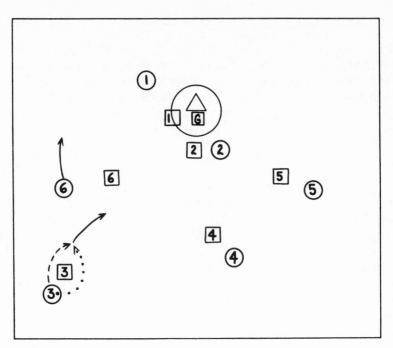

DIAGRAM 40. TOSS DODGE. ③ has the ball in mid-field. Defense 3 forces ③, who uses a toss dodge to get by his man and carries the ball in toward the goal. ① backs up behind the goal, ② plays on the crease and ④, ⑤, ⑥ draw their men out of the play.

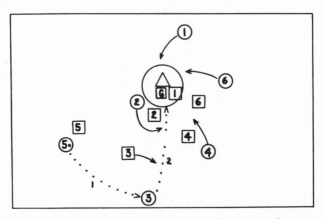

DIAGRAM 41. PASS INSTEAD OF DODGE. ⑤ notices ③ is open and passes the ball to him instead of dodging. ③ takes a shot. ① and ⑥ back up the shot. ④ closes in on the goal and ② screens.

word. However, there are many times when the best and most efficient dodges are made spontaneously, since they are initiated by the manner in which the defense man plays.

Before attempting a dodge, the player should look for someone to receive the ball after he completes the dodge, because he is usually not in the best position for a shot for goal. If he is in position, a new opponent is probably hurrying to pick him up, and he may not have time to make an accurate shot.

When a player gives the signal for a dodge, the rest of the attack players must first cover their men and then attempt to lure them away from the path of the dodger. If one defense man persists in backing up the dodger's defense man, an attack man must play near him. It is to this attack man that the dodger should pass if he is picked up before he can shoot.

Never attempt to dodge two men unless it is absolutely unavoidable. Sometimes after a player dodges, another defense man is on him so quickly that he must attempt a second dodge, since any other play is impossible. A player should dodge on the side of the field that places him in position to pass or shoot quickly and with a minimum of effort. As he faces the goal, a right-handed player should complete his dodge on the left side of the field, and a left-handed player should complete his dodge on the right side of the field. A dodge executed in back of the goal rarely results in the dodger himself obtaining the shot. Hence the dodger in this position should prepare himself ahead of time to be ready to pass to a teammate as he gets near the goal. Every attack player should be familiar with the running, force, dip, circle, and toss dodges.

For the running dodge and the force dodge, it is best to give a signal, in order that the attack men can draw their opponents away from the side of the field where the dodge is to be attempted.

Sometimes the defense men do not pull over as the attack players would have them do. In this situation, two alternatives are open. The player who had planned to dodge may pass the ball to a player left open, rather than start a dodge (see Diagram 41); or, if he makes the dodge and cannot make an immediate pass, an attack man must play near the new defense man who is preparing to intercept the dodger. When the dodger is met by this new opponent, he should pass the ball to a teammate and not attempt a shot himself (see Diagram 38).

Diagram 39 illustrates plays in which a dodger uses the force dodge. The force dodge can also be used from the side. However, the same individual should never attempt it too often in any game.

The dip dodge and the circle dodge cannot be prearranged. They are particularly effective because of the suddenness and unexpectedness of their execution. Both of these dodges must be made just at the right moment, and, if the rest of attack men are in proper formation and alert, they may well result in goals. A dip dodge is effective when an attack player finds himself being forced or rushed or sees plenty of open territory in front of the goal. He makes a dip dodge and goes on in to shoot or to pass. When an opponent rushes the man with the ball, the latter player can use the circle dodge to advantage.

The toss dodge is most effective against a defense that forces its men all over the field regardless of how far they are from the goal. It is performed to best advantage in the middle of the field, just after the ball has been recovered from the opposing team. This dodge is also useful to a defense man when clearing (see page 133). Diagram 40 illustrates the use of the toss dodge.

LONG-SHOT PLAYS

Use of the long shot does not presuppose an organized plan of attack. Any time a player with the ball, in front of the goal, sees a number of players milling around the crease, he should take a shot. As the ball comes toward the goal, the men on the crease should check their opponents' sticks *upward* in order to prevent the sticks from interfering with the path of the ball. At the same time, the man directly in the path of the ball should let it pass between his legs, thereby shielding it as much as possible from the vision of the goalkeeper. Then he should turn, facing the goal, and be prepared to make a rebound shot.

An ideal time to attempt a long shot is directly after a loose ball has been recovered by one of the midfield players in front of the goal. Just as he receives the loose ball, he calls, "Go to the crease," and a few seconds later attempts the shot. With his call, the attack immediately races for the crease. If the shot is made on a prearranged signal, one man should be on the crease directly in line with the player with the ball, and at least two other players close by, one on each side of the path the ball is to take. After the midfield player makes the shot, the two outside men cross the path of the ball just as it goes by and then turn in toward the crease. Diagram 42 illustrates the use of the long-shot play.

SET PLAYS

Lacrosse will never develop into a game in which set plays are employed throughout the entire sixty minutes. The beauty of lacrosse lies in its naturalness and in its openness. To try to fill the playing time with set plays kills the sport. The players become confused; the play, slow; and the game, uninteresting to player and spectator alike. One of the reasons for few set plays is that the players are too far apart and are rarely in the same positions for more than a few seconds at a time. Hence, too much time would be wasted while the players shifted back and forth preparing for each play. However, set plays do have a part in the game of lacrosse. Even though players may never execute them in a game, they should use them in practice and in scrimmage. Set plays help to impress the players with the need for teamwork; they teach position play and balance; and, at all times, they emphasize offensiveness.

During a game, there are certain times when the set play may be used to advantage:

1. At the start of the game, when each team is playing cautiously and each player is attempting to test his opponent's ability
2. At the start of each quarter, when the players have had a chance to talk over what they want to do
3. As a relief measure for the defense after it has had difficulty in clearing the ball (The attack wishes to give its defense a chance to rest but, at the same time, wants to attempt to score in a deliberate, methodical manner.)
4. After a goal has been scored by either team
5. At any time when the leader of the attack feels that certain of his players are becoming unduly excited (The play acts as a calming influence and yet is always an offensive gesture.)

Incidentally, if Team A agrees on a certain play before a face-off and Team B gets possession of the ball at the face-off instead of A, Team A should forget that the play was called and employ straight tactics until another opportunity offers itself.

Plays may be called in a variety of ways. One method of calling a play is by means of a *huddle* before the face-off. In the huddle, all players on the attack can plan what is going to take place without giving any warning to the opposing defense. A second method is through the use of *signals* to designate the different plays. The leader of the attack may call the play by number, by raising his arm, or by raising his stick high in the air.

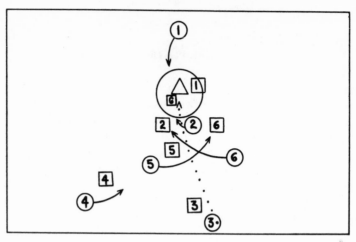

DIAGRAM 42. THE LONG SHOT. ③ has the ball and calls the signal
for a long shot. ② plays on the crease, ⑤ and ⑥ move in to a position
about three yards in front of the goal, ① backs up as ③ takes the shot,
and ④ moves in with the shot. As ③ shoots, ⑤ and ⑥ cross the path of
the ball and close in on the crease. If defense ③ forces ③ too much after
he calls the play, ③ passes to ④, cuts in fast, carrying his man with him,
stops suddenly, takes a few steps back, receives a pass from ④, and then
takes a long shot for goal.

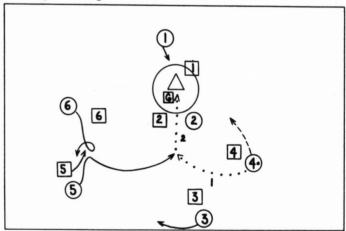

DIAGRAM 43. SIMPLE SCREEN. ④ has the ball. ⑥ cuts over and
forms a screen for ⑤, who runs around him and receives a pass from ④.
⑥ backs up the pass after ⑤ goes by. ① closes in on the rear crease circle.
② plays the crease and ③ moves over to the middle position. (In this
formation, ⑤ should be a right-handed player.)

88

Simple Screen

The simple screen is any set play that involves not more than two passes before the shot. It is important that the player making the screen stop at least a yard away from the defense man who is to be screened, in order that no foul be committed. Diagrams 43 and 44 illustrate the simple screen.

Multi-pass Screen

The multi-pass screen is any set play in which, after the play is called, more than two passes are made before the screen is executed. It is the best type of play to attempt against a forcing defense, because the passer does not have to hold the ball more than an instant, and hence the defense man does not have an opportunity to force him out of play. It is a difficult maneuver to carry out, since both timing and passing must be nearly perfect for it to succeed. This type of play is illustrated in Diagram 45.

CLOSE-ATTACK FORMATION WHILE WAITING FOR THE BALL

The close attack must be alert and watch the play while waiting for the ball and must guard against becoming too chummy with their opponents during the game. The following formations are commonly used: two men near the center line and one back, three men at the center line, and one man at the center line and two men back. Diagrams 46 to 48 illustrate these formations.

In the *two men near the center line and one back* formation, two men play on opposite sides of the field about 10 yards from the center line and about 15 yards from the side lines. These men play back from the center line in order to have room to go to meet the ball without the danger of being forced off-side. The third plays near the crease ready to go swiftly forward to obtain any loose ball. (See Diagram 46.) He moves out to either side to receive passes from his teammates. They throw the ball to him whenever possible, since he is in the best position to see and pass to any extra man who may be able to reach scoring territory. They always pass to him, except under the following four conditions: if he (the crease man) is covered; if the ball carrier feels he has an opportunity to dodge; or feels it is advantageous to pass to someone else; or is himself forced to such an extent that he has no alternative other than to run with the ball. The crease man should always face scoring terri-

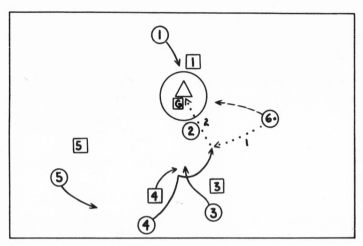

DIAGRAM 44. SIMPLE SCREEN.   ⑥ has the ball. ④ (a right-handed player) and ③ cut together toward the goal, with ④ slightly in the lead. Suddenly ④ cuts around ③, who acts as a screen for him. ⑥ gives ④ a pass and ④ shoots. ⑤ backs up the pass, ① backs up the goal, and ② plays the crease.

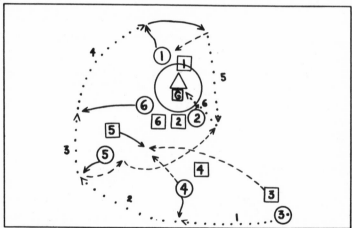

DIAGRAM 45. MULTI-PASS SCREEN.   ③ has the ball. ④ cuts in to draw his man out of the play then cuts out to receive a pass from ③. ⑤ cuts out to receive a pass from ④. ⑥ cuts out to receive a pass from ⑤ and then passes to ①. As ⑥ passes to ①, ③ and ④ screen for ⑤, who cuts around them to receive a pass from ① and shoot. After ① passes to ⑤, he backs up behind the goal and ② plays the crease. The purpose in the attack men cutting first in and then out is to prevent their opponents from interfering with the play.

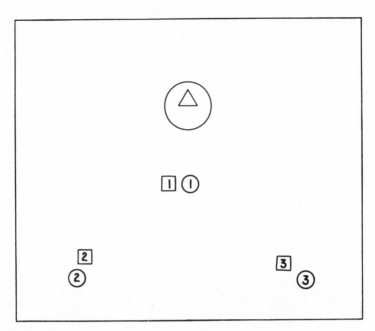

DIAGRAM 46. CLOSE-ATTACK FORMATION WHILE WAITING FOR THE BALL.
A. Two Near Center Line and One Back.

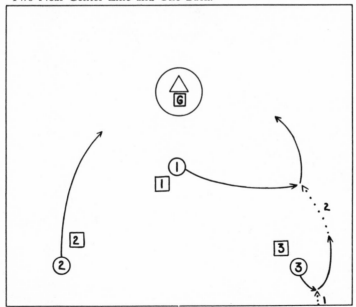

B. ③ receives the ball, which has just come across the center line and, turning, passes to ①, who has run out to meet the ball. ② races for the crease and ① turns facing scoring territory.

tory when he gets the ball, because, if the ball reaches him before the rest of the players get up the field, the three close-attack men may find opportunities for cut and pass plays or dodging.

When the ball comes on the ground toward either of the two men at the center line, they are often unable to get it cleanly because of the interference of the defense men covering them. In this case, they should not play the ball at all but should prevent their defense men from getting the ball. The proper method of play here is for the attack man to get his stick under his opponent's and lift it just as the ball reaches him, permitting the ball to roll on down the field (see Figure 22). It is the duty of the crease man to get the ball; if he is asleep at his post or talking to his opponent, it may be disastrous for his team.

FIGURE 22. LIFTING THE STICK AT THE CENTER LINE. (Black, the attack, spoils the opponent's play by lifting White's stick so the ball rolls.)

In the *three men at the center line* formation, all three play parallel to the center line and about 10 yards from it (see Diagram 47). This is a particularly effective formation if the defense play man for man and cover their opponents regardless of where they go. For now when one of the close-attack men receives the ball he has an excellent opportunity to outrun his check to the goal for a free shot. However, passes made up the field must not be thrown too hard, or the goalkeeper will be able to recover a ball that gets by the waiting players. As a ground ball comes toward him, the attacking player lifts his opponent's stick, lets the ball go by, then turns swiftly, recovers the ball, and races for the goal. Of course, if he feels he can play the ground ball cleanly, he does so.

In the *one man up and two back* formation, one man plays in the middle of the field about 10 yards from the center line, while the other two men play back near the crease, about 20 yards apart. Diagram 48 illustrates this formation. The man in the middle of the field roves back and forth across the field, playing on the side with the ball as it is being cleared. The other two players must be ready to come quickly forward to receive a pass or to pick up a loose ball. While this formation has the advantage that the men have plenty of room to come to meet the ball, it must not be used unless the defense men play back with the attack men. Otherwise the defense men will have the advantage when playing a loose ball or going forward to intercept a pass.

RIDING THE DEFENSE

As soon as the defense players get possession of the ball, they attempt to get it to their attack. This is called *clearing*. At the same time the opposing attack men attempt to prevent the defense men from clearing the ball. This is called *riding*. In theory, the defense men, because they have an extra man (the goalkeeper), should be able to clear the ball to their attack every time. In practice, because the attack men overcome the advantage of the extra defense man by means of speed and aggressiveness, clears are not always successful.

There are several different methods of riding the defense. In using these, the attack must be sure not to override the man with the ball. Overriding is known as *rushing*. If this takes place, the defense man can easily elude the rider and carry the ball on up the field.

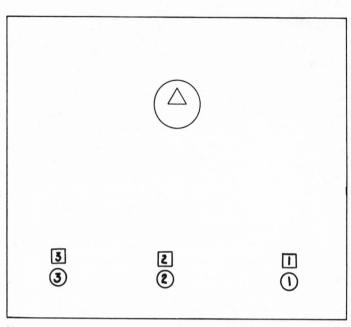

DIAGRAM 47.   THREE MEN AT THE CENTER LINE.

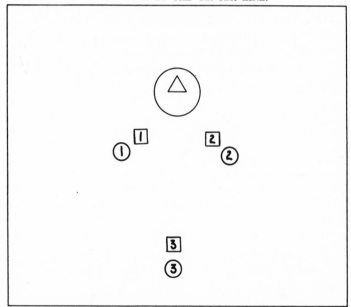

DIAGRAM 48.   ONE MAN UP AND TWO BACK.

Man-to-Man Ride

In the man-to-man ride, one attack man plays the defense man with the ball as hard as he can without overplaying him. The other defense men near the ball carrier are also covered by attack players. As the man with the ball goes to pass, his opponent rides him. The attack man should have his stick raised and in line with the passer's stick to attempt to block the pass. (See Diagram 49.)

Zone Ride

In the zone ride, the progress of the defense man with the ball is not impeded until the ball carrier approaches the center line. When the defense gains possession of the ball behind the goal, the attack men race toward the center line and line up in two rows of three each. One set of three players plays close to the center line, and the other group plays about 15 yards in front of them. As the defense men bring the ball up the field, the first three attack men pick up the ball carrier and the two defense men nearest to him. The purpose of the zone ride is to bewilder the defense men—to keep them from finding an opening quickly. If they become confused and do not use the goalkeeper as their extra man, the attack generally recovers the ball. The zone is an effective ride provided the opposing team has not had a chance to practice against it. However, it retards the action of the game and is not practical for a team that is behind in score. (See Diagram 50.)

Two Men Cover the Man with the Ball

Another style of ride sometimes employed is for two attack men to play the man with the ball while the other attack men cover the men closest to the ball carrier. This is an excellent and extremely effective ride if the two riding the ball carrier are able to reach him soon enough to prevent him from passing. However, if they do not, the defense has two extra men instead of just one and the chances for the attack to prevent a clear are much slimmer. (See Diagram 51.)

Standard Ride

Another example of a ride when the clear starts behind the goal is the standard ride, which is illustrated in Diagram 52—A, B, C. As the goalie carries the ball behind the goal, the nearest close-attack

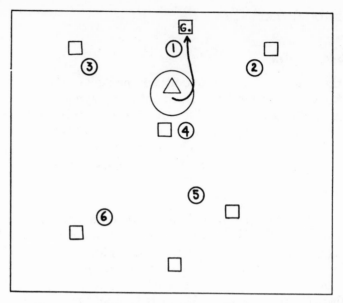

DIAGRAM 49. MAN-TO-MAN RIDE.   The goalkeeper has carried the ball behind the goal. ① rides the goalie. ②, ③ and ④ cover the men near the man with the ball. ⑤ and ⑥ drop back, ready to play the closest men to the ball-carrier as the ball is passed up the field.

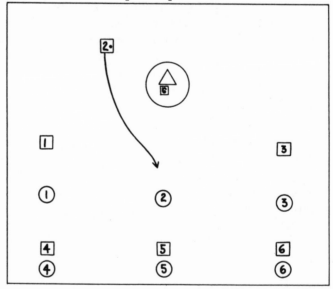

DIAGRAM 50. ZONE RIDE.   ② will pick up the man with the ball, ① and ③ will pick up the men closest to the ball-carrier. ④, ⑤ and ⑥ are responsible for the next three defense players.

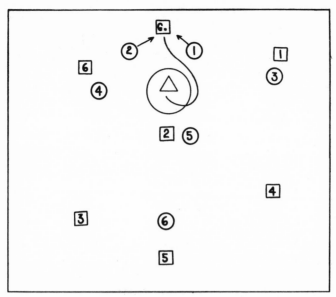

DIAGRAM 51.   TWO MEN COVER THE MAN WITH THE BALL.   ① and ②
play the defense man with the ball. ③, ④ and ⑤ cover the men closest
to the ball-carrier. ⑥ drops back to intercept any pass that the ball-carrier
may make up-field.

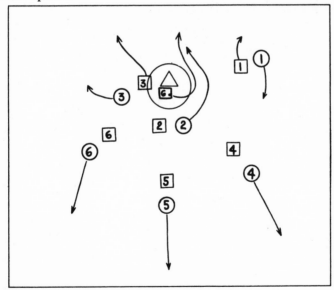

DIAGRAM 52.   STANDARD RIDE.
A.   The goalkeeper carries the ball behind the goal preparing to clear. ② plays
him hard. ① and ③ move to positions on either side of the goal until the goalkeeper makes his first pass. ④, ⑤ and ⑥ run toward the center line, stopping
some 15 yards before reaching it.

97

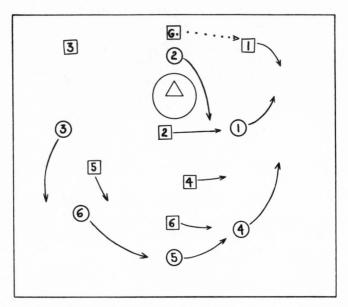

DIAGRAM 52.

B. The goalkeeper passes to the man on his right. ① immediately plays him hard. ② moves up the field on the ball side. ④, ⑤ and ⑥ move over to the ball side to prevent the defense from clearing on that side. ③ runs fast toward the center line to intercept any long pass across the field.

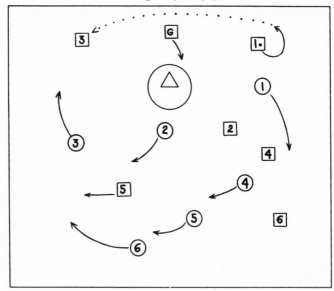

C. ① reverses the direction of the ball and passes to ③; ③ rides him hard. ②, ④, ⑤ and ⑥ shift over to the ball side, and ① drifts up the right side.

player rides him hard but must not override him. The three mid-fielders break for the center line, and the other two close-attack men move out a short distance on either side of the goal. As the clear develops up one side, the close-attack man on that side plays the man that receives the first pass. The entire midfield pulls over to that side, covering any possible pass receivers. The close-attack man on the other side goes up the field to prevent a possible pass across the field.

EXTRA MAN

Sometimes during a game of lacrosse a player on Team B is ejected from the game because of some infraction of the rules. This expulsion may last from thirty seconds for a very minor infraction to three minutes for a serious offense. Or possibly a defense man on Team A has obtained possession of the ball and been able to carry it to his attack a few steps ahead of his opponent. In either case, Team A has the advantage of having one more attacking player than Team B and, hence, is said to have an *extra* man. In the following sections, both situations are discussed from the attack point of view.

Four-Against-Three Play

Sometimes a defense man on Team A gets the ball and finds the opportunity to break quickly up the field ahead of his opponents, with the intent of getting the ball to his own attack players. As he crosses the center line with the ball, he becomes an extra man, and, together with his three attack players, can set up a four-against-three play. The attack on Team A must place themselves in advantageous positions so as to be able to receive passes from each other preparatory to taking a shot at the goal. If no member of Team B picks up the extra Team A defense man, he carries the ball as close to the goal as possible and takes a shot himself. As he comes up the field, his close-attack men, playing near the center line, drop back. (See Diagram 53. Note that, in B, C, and D, after 4 makes his first pass, he goes no closer to the goal. He remains alert for a possible return pass from one of his teammates.)

Practice the four-against-three setup extensively in order that both attack and defense may become familiar with their parts. Incidentally, the farther out from the goal the defense checks the extra man, the more chance there is for success in the play, since there is greater opportunity for the attack men to make good passes.

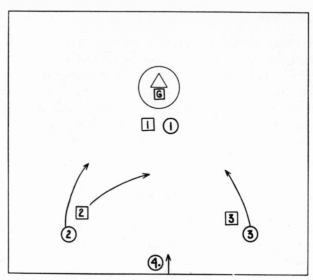

DIAGRAM 53. FOUR-AGAINST-THREE PLAY WITH TWO UP AND ONE BACK.
A. ④ (Team A defense) carries the ball across the center line. ④ is an extra man. ② and ③ drop back toward the goal and ① stays on the crease. Thus Team A sets up a four-against-three (opponents) situation. ② goes toward center of field preparatory to taking ④.

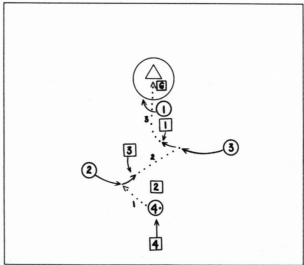

B. ② takes ④, forcing him to pass. ② receives the pass. ③ checks ② so ② passes to ③, who shoots. ① covers the crease. (If ② is close enough to the goal after he receives the pass from ④, he shoots. If ③ picks up ④, the first pass from ④ goes to ③ and the play is reversed.)

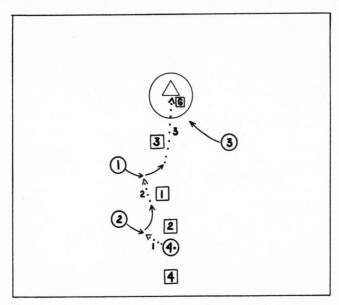

C. 2 picks up ④ and forces a pass. ④ passes to ②, who comes to meet the ball. 1 picks up ②. ② passes to ①, who shoots. ③ goes to the crease as ① shoots. (If ① is covered, he passes to ③ as illustrated in D.)

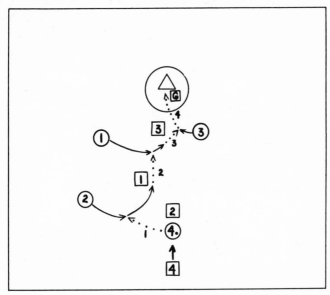

D. 2 picks up ④, who passes to ②. 1 picks up ②, who passes to ①. 3 comes to take ①, so ① passes to ③, who shoots.

101

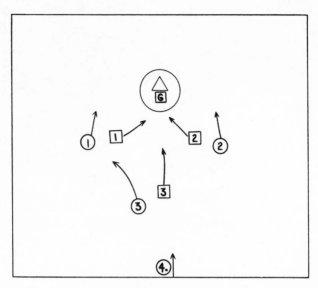

DIAGRAM 54. FOUR-AGAINST-THREE PLAY WITH TWO BACK AND ONE UP.
A. ④ comes up the field with the ball, as an extra man. ① and ② drop
back to positions parallel to the front of the goal and about 10 yards on
either side of it. ③ comes back with his defense man and plays parallel
with him and about 5 yards away from him. (If possible ③ should be able
to pass and soot from either side. He should draw over to the left side of ④
if ④ is right-handed and to his right side if ④ is left-handed.)

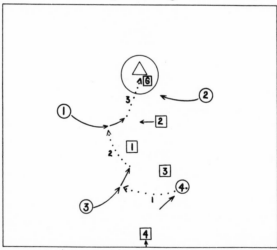

B. As ③ takes ④, ③ should be in a position to go to meet the ball and
to see both ① and ②. ④ passes to ③. ① takes ③, so ③ passes to ①, who
shoots. ② comes in to the crease. (If ② takes ① before he can shoot, he
passes to ②. ④ does not advance after he makes his pass to ③.)

102

So, if the attack player is clever enough to maneuver his opponent into checking the extra man far out, it is decidedly to his advantage.

When the close-attack men use the formation of two back and one up (see page 93), the four-against-three play develops as illustrated in Diagram 54.

Man Out of the Game

The second type of extra-man play develops when a player is ejected from the game due to an infraction of the rules. This sets up an entirely different situation from the four-against-three play, which happens quickly, with no time for organization. When an opponent leaves the field, the attack players have an opportunity to organize, and it is tremendously important that they take advantage of this opportunity. The play should be deliberate; it is better to take time to set up a formation for one good, hard, direct shot at the goal before the banished player returns than it is to take several wild shots that are nowhere near the goal. Several formations are suggested in Diagrams 55 to 57—A and B.

ATTACK FORMATIONS

The most common formation used by attack players entails having two men behind the goal, one man on the crease, and the three midfielders in front of the goal (see Diagram 58 A). When this formation is used, it is customary for the same man to play the crease at all times. The ball is passed back and forth behind the goal while the midfielders take their turns at screening for each other as they cut for passes.

Another formation sometimes used requires three men behind the goal, one man on the crease, and two midfielders in front of the goal (see Diagram 58 B). The three attack men are behind the goal, and one of the midfielders plays on the crease. Unless a team has midfielders capable of exceptional stickwork, it is not advisable to attempt this formation. However, the advantages in having the attack play this way follow:

1. It puts on the crease a defensive player, who, as a general rule, is unaccustomed to the position.
2. It brings three defense men behind the goal and thus enlarges the scoring territory in front of the goal.
3. It puts four attack men close to the crease circle and makes it more difficult for the goalie to get clear.

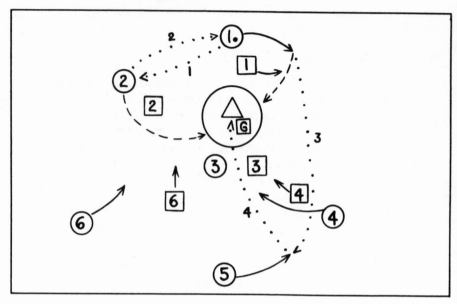

DIAGRAM 55. FORMATION FOR EXTRA-MAN PLAY. As soon as the whistle blows to start the game after the penalty, the ball is passed to ① behind the goal. The players assume a balanced formation about the goal. (Bear in mind that the numbers have no particular significance.) After ① has the ball, he passes to ② in order to draw two defense men behind the goal. (If they do not come back then, ① and ② should start to come around the goal with the ball and thereby force two defense men to play them.) When the defense men (⊡ and ☒), have come back ① calls, "Cut." ④ and ⑥ now race toward the crease calling for a pass. Two of the defense men should follow them, leaving ⑤ open. ⑤ cuts out slightly to the right, receives a pass from ①, and takes a shot for goal. After ① passes, he comes in close to the goal, as does ②. If ① is forced so vigorously that it is impossible for him to make the pass, ② makes it. ② can play on either side of the goal. Whenever possible the men should be placed so that they can shoot for the goal with the least possible waste of time or energy.

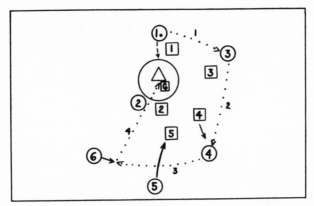

DIAGRAM 56. FORMATION FOR EXTRA-MAN PLAY. As soon as the players are in balanced formation and ① has the ball back of goal, ① passes to ③, who in turn passes to ④. As soon as ④ gets the ball, ⑤ cuts for the crease, hoping to carry the last defense man in with him. ⑥ comes toward ④, receives a pass and takes a shot. ② stays on the crease and screens the goalkeeper from the shot. ① goes to the rear of the crease after he passes to ③.

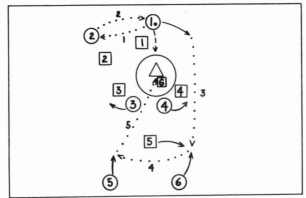

DIAGRAM 57. FORMATION FOR EXTRA-MAN PLAY.
A. ① and ② play behind the goal, ③ and ④ play on the crease, and ⑤ and ⑥ play about 10 yards in front of the goal. ① has the ball. He passes to ② to draw his defense man back. ② passes back to ①. When the defense have come back, ① calls, "Cut," and ③ and ④ move quickly to opposite corners of the crease. ① passes to any one of the four players who is open. If ⑤ and ⑥ are both right-handed and ③ and ④ are covered, the pass should go to ⑥, and when the defense man takes him, he flicks a pass to ⑤, who takes the shot. (If one defense man thinks he can play both ③ and ④ (since they are close together), when ① calls, "Cut," this defense man will follow ③ or ④, leaving the other open for a very close shot.)

105

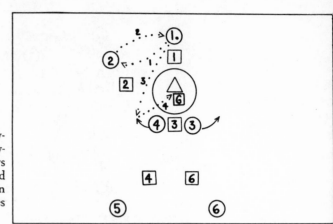

DIAGRAM 57.
B. If ⑤ and ⑥ are covered, the defense man playing both ③ and ④ follows ③. ④ gets the pass and shoots. (If the defense man follows ④, the pass goes to ③.)

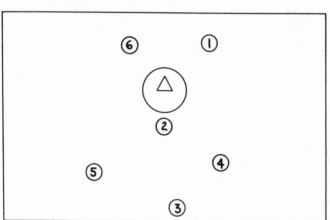

DIAGRAM 58. ATTACK FORMATIONS.
A. Two Men Back of Goal.

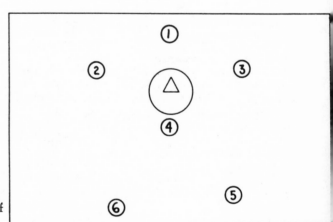

B. Three Men Back of Goal.

As the offense begins, the ball is taken behind the goal and passed rapidly back and forth until one of the three attack men sees an opportunity to cut around the goal. If he has the ball in his possession, he either attempts a shot or passes to one of the three men in front of the goal. If he does not have the ball, he uses the crease man as a screen and hopes to be extra in front of the goal. His teammate with the ball should be ready to pass to him. The play is illustrated in Diagram 59.

ATTACK AGAINST THE ZONE SYSTEM OF DEFENSE

Sometimes a team employs a zone defense against the attack. This is described in detail from the defensive point of view in Chapter 7. In brief, it means that each defense man has a certain territory to cover rather than a specific player (see page 143). This section explains how an attack should operate in order to break through the zone.

The method is very simple and consists of two parts: (1) short, quick passes and (2) a fast-moving attack. The passes should be short, to prevent interception, and thrown rapidly back and forth behind the goal and around the outside, so that each defense man must turn continually with the ball and, therefore, be unable to concentrate on what is taking place in his territory. In this way, too, the ball can be worked close to the rear of the goal. After the ball is carried close to the rear crease line, the various attack men take their turns at cutting quickly for the goal. When one is open, he receives a quick pass from behind the goal and shoots for goal. If he is not open, he circles back quickly to a position in front of the goal and a teammate cuts. If this style is methodically followed, the attack should be able to keep possession of the ball and score. There is no point in dodging against a zone, since the defense men are all fairly close together and the dodger can be checked hard before he has a chance to pass or shoot. Diagram 60 (pages 109–111) illustrates an attack operating against a zone defense.

EXERCISES

Exercise 1 (illustrated)

Formation. Players in a line about 15 yards in front of the left side of the goal. One player has the ball behind the goal.
Objective. To practice receiving, shooting, passing, backing up.

Procedure. Man behind the goal passes to the first in line, who runs to meet the ball and takes a shot at the goal. Passer backs up the shot, and second man in line backs up the receiver. Passer takes his place at the end of the line. The shooter goes behind the goal to become the next passer. (See Diagram 61.)
Variations. (1) Have the players assemble on the opposite side of the goal, and also directly in the center. Have the passer take different positions behind the goal. (2) Assemble the players in back of the goal, and place the passer in front of the goal.

Exercise 2 (*illustrated*)

Formation. Two lines of ten players about 15 yards in front of the goal, with the passer located behind the goal. Place the lines about 10 yards apart.
Objective. To practice receiving, screening, passing, backing up, and shooting.
Procedure. The first man in line A screens for the first man in line B. As player from line B goes by, he receives a pass from the player behind the goal and takes a shot. Second man in line B backs up the pass. The shooter then becomes the passer, and the passer goes to the end of line A while the screener goes to the end of line B. (See Diagram 62.)
Variations. (1) Have players in line B screen for the players in line A. (2) Put the two lines in back of, and on either side of, the goal and the passer in front of the goal.

Exercise 3

Formation. Six players in balanced formation around the goal— two men in back of the goal, one man on the crease, and three men in front.
Objective. To practice passing, backing up, screening, cutting, shooting, and keeping a balanced formation.
Procedure. Pass the ball back and forth, with different players taking their turns at cutting and screening.
Variation. Put three men back and two men in front.

Exercise 4 (*illustrated*)

Formation. Two lines of ten players, each line 15 yards in front of the goal. Place the lines about 10 yards apart. First player in line B has the ball.

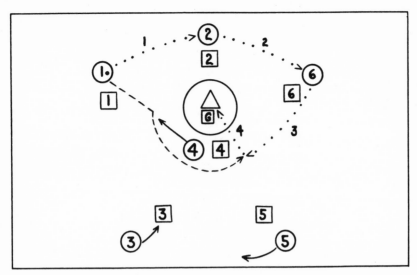

DIAGRAM 59. ATTACK PLAY. ① passes to ②. As ② passes to ⑥, ①
cuts around the goal to receive a pass from ⑥. ④ backs up to screen for
①. ③ moves in and backs up the pass from ⑥, and ⑤ covers the center-
front position.

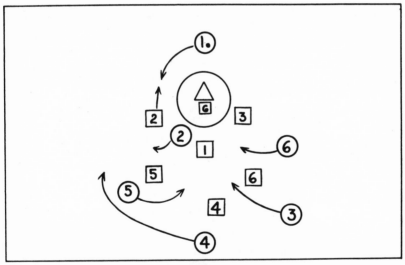

DIAGRAM 60. ATTACK AGAINST THE ZONE SYSTEM OF DEFENSE.
A. ① has the ball behind the goal. The attack closes in. ① carries the
ball around the goal and may get a shot. If ② takes ①, ② may be left
open. If ② is not open, ④ may brush off of ⑤ and be open.

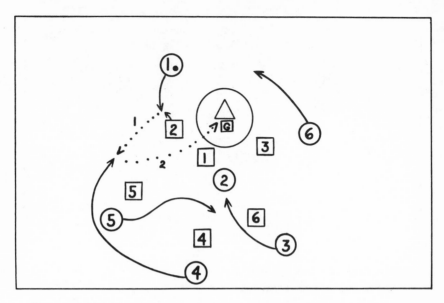

DIAGRAM 60. B. ① passes to ④, who shoots. ⑥ backs up the shot, and ③ moves in toward the goal. ② stays on the crease. ⑤ plays the center position after ④ goes by.

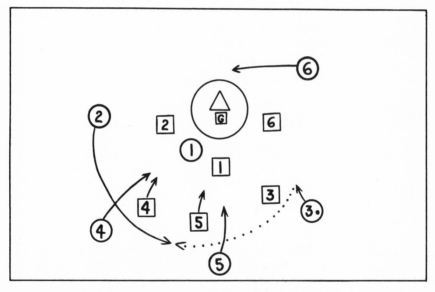

C. ③ has the ball, guarded by ③. ④ and ⑤ cut toward the crease, and ② drifts to the right. ② may be open for a pass.

110

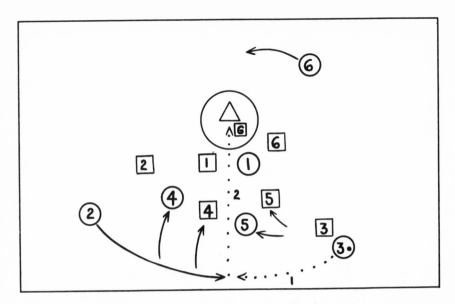

D.   As ④ and ⑤ cut toward the crease, ④ and ⑤ start back with them. ② plays the zone and does not come over as ② drifts to the right. ③ passes to ② who takes a shot at the goal.

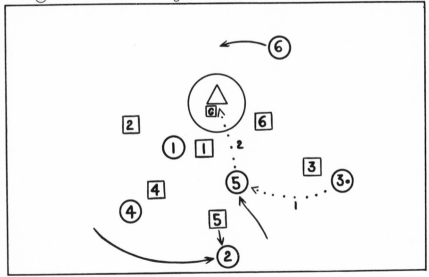

E.   ⑤ picks up ②, ③ passes to ⑤. If ④ is close enough, he should check ④'s stick as ③ passes.

111

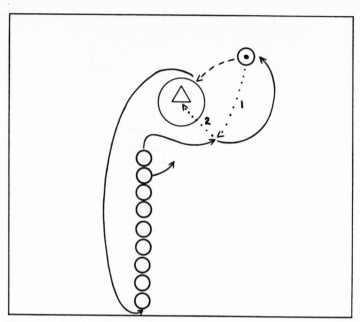

DIAGRAM 61. EXERCISE 1.

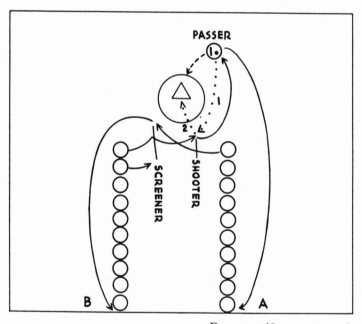

DIAGRAM 62. EXERCISE 2.

112

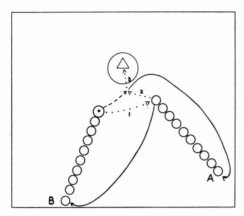

DIAGRAM 63.   EXERCISE 4.

Objective. To pass and cut and shoot.

Procedure. Player in line B passes the ball to player in line A and then cuts for the goal. Player in A returns the pass, and player in B takes a shot. After the shot, the two players take their places at the ends of opposite lines. (See Diagram 63.)

Variations. (1) Have the ball start in the possession of player in line A. (2) Place both lines in back of the goal.

7

STRATEGY OF DEFENSE

Just as the attack players are the men who must score the goals, so the defense players are the men responsible for keeping goals from being scored. In many respects this is a much more difficult task, since they must anticipate what their opponents are planning to do. A mistake on their part can be fatal and lead to a score. Team play is extremely essential.

Fundamentals of defense have already been discussed from an individual point of view, and now the defense player is ready to learn to play the game. He must learn how to clear, what to do against an extra man, where to play while waiting for the ball. These and other things important in defense strategy are discussed in this chapter.

PLAYING THE POSITION

While the attack players have the ball, the defense must always be ready for a pass and cut play, a screen play, or a dodge, and should place themselves so as to frustrate any style of offense.

During the Attack

The defense player who is covering the man with the ball must devote his entire attention to his man. The other defense men should try to guard their men, watch the ball, and be ready to offer assistance to a teammate in trouble. As the ball is passed from one side of the goal to the other, the defense men should move back and forth, going out toward their men on the side where the ball is and dropping in closer to the goal on the other side. This enables them to be ready to pick up a dodger and to intercept many passes. Diagram 64 illustrates this.

While Waiting for the Ball

Regardless of how the attack plays, the defense always keeps at least one man back near the goal. If the entire attack formation is playing back, the defense must, of course, play back with them. When the attack formation has two men near the center line and one man back near the goal (see page 89), the defense must cover all three closely. As an opponent passes the ball toward the center line, up one side of the field, the defense man on that side plays the opponents' attack man closely, attempting to prevent him from catching the ball. When the attack throws the ball up the field on the ground, the defense man plays the ball and tries either to intercept it or to keep it from crossing the center line. Since a defense stick is usually longer than an attack stick, many times a defense man can intercept a ball before it crosses the center line and knock it back "on-side," thereby enabling his own attack to recover the ball. If the attack player is able to lift the defense man's stick to prevent his doing this, the latter attempts to kick the ball back across the center line.

In the meantime, the defense player on the other side of the field, regardless of what his opponent does, runs back toward the goal, thus freeing the defense player on the crease to follow his attack man and take an even chance of getting a loose ball, of intercepting a pass, or of preventing his man from receiving the ball. There should always be a defense man near the crease ready to play any extra man from the attack who might have dodged into the clear.

Sometimes an attack places three men near the center line (see page 89). In this case, the defense plays two men midway between the three players and one man back near the crease line. As the ball is thrown up the field, the man waiting to receive it and the next nearest man can easily be covered. The defense man playing back can come forward to pick up a possible loose ball and is in position to prevent any attack player from becoming an extra man. (See Diagram 65.)

The defense players who are playing up near the center line cover the men nearest to the ball closely and try to prevent them

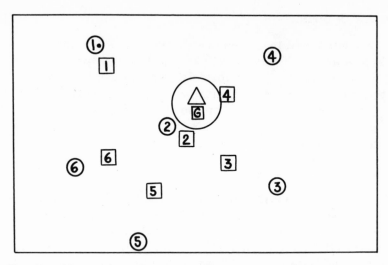

DIAGRAM 64. POSITION OF DEFENSE DURING THE ATTACK.

A. [1] forces (1), who has the ball; [2] covers the crease man (2) closely; [6] plays within a few yards of (6), since he is on the ball side, while [3], [4] and [5] drop back near the goal.

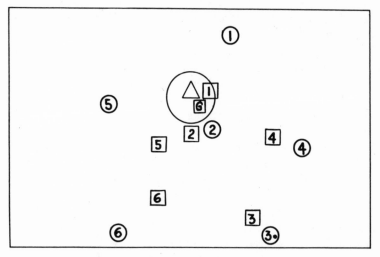

B. [3] forces (3), who has the ball. [2] covers the crease man, (2). [4] plays within a few yards of (4) since he is on the ball side, and [1], [5] and [6] drop back toward the goal.

116

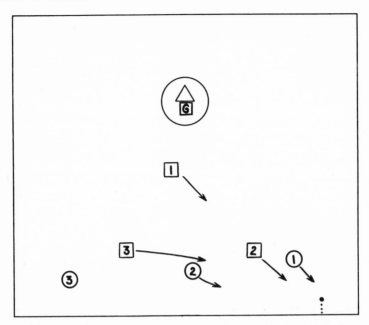

DIAGRAM 65. DEFENSE AGAINST THREE ATTACK MEN NEAR CENTER LINE.
The ball is coming up the right side of the field. ① runs toward the center
line to receive it. ② covers ①, ③ covers ②, and ① moves toward the
right side ready to play a possible loose ball.

from getting possession of it. However, if the defense sights an extra
man coming up the field, or if one of the close-attack players catches
the ball, the defense players drop back immediately. It is dangerous for the defense to check in the middle of the field, because a
skilful dodger or a fast runner can go by his man easily, and there
will be no one near enough to pick him up quickly. However, if a
team is behind in the score, there are times when players must take
chances in order to get possession of the ball. During these times,
it may be necessary for the defense to check all over the field—to
play close beside the opponent wherever he goes.

SWITCHING

With rare exceptions, the defense players should not switch their
positions to pick up a teammate's opponent. It is a dangerous type
of defense play. It disconcerts the defense and causes confusion.
Smart attack players often plan their play to force the defense play-

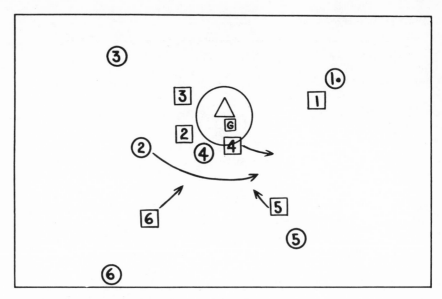

DIAGRAM 66. THE SWITCH.
A. ① has the ball. ④ stops behind ②, ② cuts around ④ to get free for a pass from ①. ②, realizing he is screened from the play, calls, "Switch," to his teammate ④. ④ now plays ②, while ② immediately plays ④. ③, ⑤ and ⑥ drop back closer to the goal.

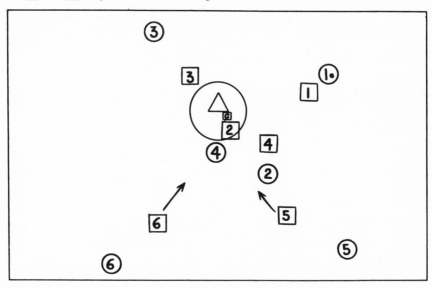

B. ④ plays ② and ② plays ④. Everybody is covered.

118

ers to switch. Two defense men find themselves playing the same attack man, while the other attack player gets open for a pass and a shot. Suddenly an inexperienced defense man finds himself pitted against a good dodger.

However, there are times when a switch must be called. The weight of the responsibility for the switch rests upon the defense man whose opponent has eluded him. Sometimes it is not the player guarding the ball carrier who gives the command for the switch. This is all right. The important thing is that the players know who is responsible for the signal for the interchange and that the person responsible knows when to call it. It is the duty of this player to call, "Take my man," or, "Switch," or words to that effect. With this signal, the remaining defense men spring into action. The teammate directly involved in the play must pick up the loose man, while the rest of the defense men drop back closer to the goal and immediately adjust themselves to the new situation. Screen plays on the part of the attack often force the defense men to switch from one opponent to another. As soon as a defense player realizes that he is going to be blocked out of a play and can no longer guard his man, he calls, "Switch," and the nearest teammate picks up this man, while the man who gave the call plays the attack man who caused the screen. (See Diagrams 66 and 67.) Remember that the num- bered defense players in the diagrams may be *any* defense players. However, in most cases defense players 1, 2, and 4 are the close- defense men, and defense players 3, 5, and 6 are the midfielders.

When an attack man with the ball starts behind the goal and attempts to run by his check, he often appears to be open although he is not. Too often another defense man gets excited and rushes to intercept this supposedly open man, with the result that the attack man executes a shovel pass to his now unguarded teammate, who shoots for goal. This situation can be averted in the following way: First, the defense man playing the ball carrier talks. If he feels sure he has the situation under control, he keeps saying, "I've got him. I've got him," or words to that effect. Second, the man guarding the attack man on the crease, hearing this, does not leave his man. Third, the midfield men automatically arrange themselves in an off- balance formation, prepared for any emergency. The midfielder closest to the play also talks, advising his teammate who is guarding the man with the ball that he is prepared to back him up.

If a defense man playing the ball carrier calls, "Pick up my man," a switch is necessary; if he does not say anything, a switch may or may not be necessary. In the latter case, the midfielder backing up the play must use his own judgment as to whether or not he should leave his man, and the other midfielders must be ready for the play. Diagram 68 further explains the technique of the play. The weight of the responsibility for the switch rests with the defense player who feels the man he is covering has escaped him. After a switch has been made, the defense men should hold their new positions until they can change back without endangering the play—until the ball goes out of bounds or is carried to the other end of the field.

PICKING UP THE EXTRA MAN

A difficult question asked by defense men is this: "When should a defense player leave the man he is covering to pick up an extra man (a man who has eluded his check) who is coming toward the goal with the ball?" This question has no definite answer. As a general rule, the defense man endeavors to time his switch so that the man with the ball is undecided whether to pass or to shoot, and to force him to pass or shoot during that moment of uncertainty.

Four Against Three

Occasionally, a defense or midfield player gets the opportunity to carry the ball up the field as an extra man. This sets up a situation of four attack men against three defense men (see page 99). The three close-defense men drop back toward their goal; then one of them, directed by the goalkeeper, must come forward and check the extra man. The other two defense men must prevent the three remaining attack men from scoring. They must force the play to such an extent that attack passes and shots are made under pressure and hence are hurried and inaccurate. Diagram 69 illustrates a progressive defense against the extra man.

Practice the four-against-three play often to enable the close-defense men to get the proper timing and to enable each man to know exactly what he is expected to do.

Picking Up the Dodger

Whenever an attack man has the ball, the defense men must be on the alert for a dodge. When it comes, they must react quickly and in perfect harmony, with timing playing a vital part. If the attempted dodge is of the deliberate type, the defense men have time to get set for it and the attack should never score a goal. The defense man who comes forward to pick up the dodger must be cer-

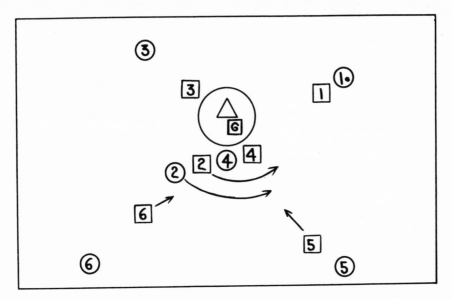

DIAGRAM 67. UNNECESSARY SWITCH.

A. ① has the ball and ② breaks for a pass. ④ attempts to screen ②, who is covering ②. ② eludes the screen and continues to play ②. ④ and ② do not switch.

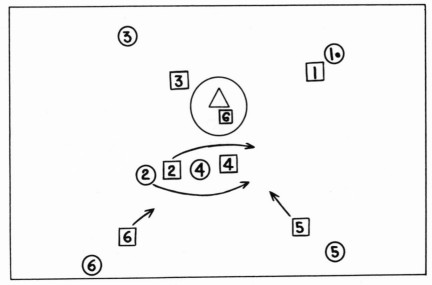

B. ① has the ball. ② breaks for a pass. ④ tries to screen ②, who eludes him by going behind him and picking up ②. Therefore, ④ and ② do not switch.

See C next page.

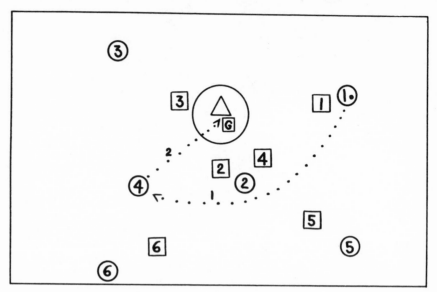

DIAGRAM 67. C. 4 switches without informing 2 (see B). 4 and 2 cover ② leaving ④ open. ① passes to ④, who shoots for goal. 4 should not have switched without a signal from 2.

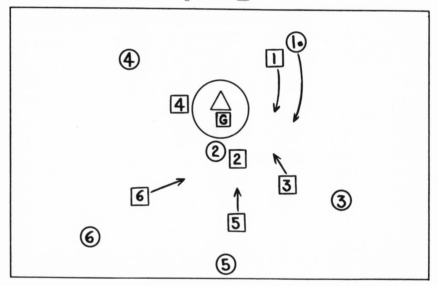

DIAGRAM 68. THE SWITCH.
A. ① runs with the ball. 1 stays with him and keeps saying, "I've got him." 2 does not leave ② at the crease to pick up ①. Neither does 3 pick up ①. 3 drops back toward the crease, ready for any emergency. 4, 5 and 6 all drop back toward the goal.

122

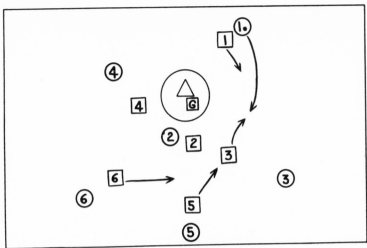

B. ① goes by ①, who calls, "Pick him up!" ③, who has dropped back, picks up ①. ⑤ switches over to play ③. ⑥ moves over between ⑤ and ⑥. ① comes back to the crease as quickly as possible and picks up ⑥. ② plays his man tight.

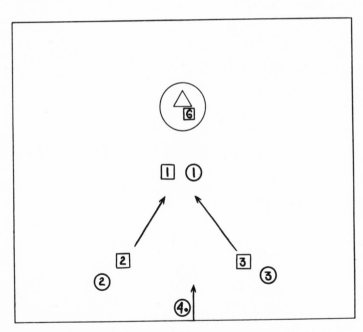

DIAGRAM 69. FOUR-AGAINST-THREE PLAY.
A. ② and ③ drop back fast as they see ④ coming in extra.

123

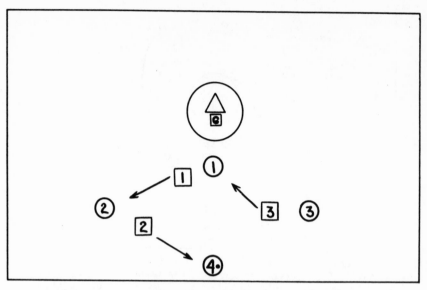

B. [2], ordered by the goalie, takes the extra man, ④. [1] and [3] shift to ② and ①, respectively, leaving ③ uncovered. If [3] had been ordered to take the extra man, the situation would be reversed.

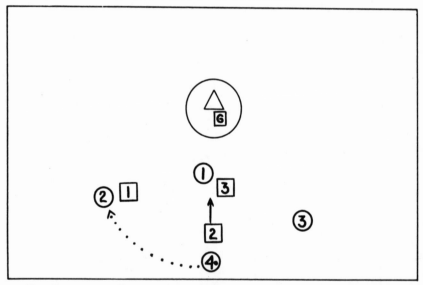

C. ④ passes to ②. Immediately after the pass [2] drops back facing the ball side. If [2] does not pick up the extra man too far out from the goal and crease he will be much more effective in assisting his teammates when he drops back after the first pass. [2] may be able to intercept a pass to ③.

124

tain that he makes a play for the body of his opponent and not just for the stick. He must hit the dodger hard just as he goes by so that the dodger does not have time to shoot or make a pass. (See Diagram 70.)

The instantaneous dodge by an attack man is dangerous for the defense man, because it is apt to catch him unprepared. The defense man closest to the dodger must play him to the best of his ability, remembering to play the body as well as the stick. The case where the dodger goes by his defense man from behind the goal and becomes an extra man is illustrated in Diagrams 68 A and B.

Sometimes it is necessary for the goalie to leave his goal and check the extra man. The goalie must time his maneuver perfectly, so that he makes his check as the extra man is about to catch the ball. Diagram 71 illustrates situations where the goalie takes the extra. These are risky plays for the goalkeeper, and chances for success are favorable only if the attack player who receives the pass is fairly close to the goal.

Men Out of the Game

Whenever the attack has more players on the field owing to a penalty against the defense, the defense must readjust itself rapidly. If the defense has *one man* out of the game, the players can force the opposing attack. One defense player must force the man with the ball in order to prevent him from making a good pass; the rest of the defense must drop back close to the goal. As soon as the attack makes a pass, some defense player must immediately pick up the receiver of the pass and start forcing him. The defense player whose opponent passed must drop back immediately to a position close to the goal. (See Diagram 72.)

When the defense has *two men* out of the game, they must not attempt to force the man with the ball. The play now is to form a square (two men on either side of the crease circle and two about 5 yards directly in front of them) in front of the goal and wait for the attack to come in with the ball. As the attack passes the ball around, the defense must hold their positions and not allow themselves to be drawn out. The ball carrier must be checked just as he is about to take a shot. (See Diagram 73.) If a defense player recovers the ball and sees his way clear to carry the ball up the field, he should do so. Ordinarily the best way for a defense player to clear in this situation is to throw the ball far up the field to the waiting attack.

On rare occasions, the defense has *three men* out of the game. When this situation happens, the defense must form a triangle in front of the goal: two men on either side of the crease circle and one man about 5 yards directly in front of the goal. They must, again, wait for the attack to come to them and attempt to check the ball carrier as he is about to take a shot at the goal. (See Diagram 74.) If a defense player recovers the ball, the best way for him to clear is to throw the ball far up the field to the waiting attack, unless he sees a chance to carry the ball out of danger himself.

CLEARING

The defense has two important duties to perform: to take the ball away from the opposing attack and to get the ball up to its own attack. This second duty is called *clearing* and often is the more difficult of the two assignments.

With a Fast Break

When a defense player intercepts a pass from the opposing attack (see Diagram 75) or recovers a loose ball (see Diagram 76) near the attack's goal, he must break for open territory and carry the ball up the field at top speed. This type of clearing often results in a four-against-three setup at the other end of the field (see page 99).

Whenever a defense man gets possession of the ball and breaks into open territory, his two nearest teammates must spread rapidly to either side of him to open the play and to receive a possible pass. The ball carrier may be able (1) to pass directly up the field; (2) by turning properly, to make a long pass to a teammate on the opposite side of the field; or (3) to pass the ball around behind the goal and then up on the opposite side. Diagram 77 illustrates a few of the various situations that may develop.

From Behind the Goal

When the goalkeeper gets possession of the ball and an attack man is on the crease, it is often expedient for the goalie to run around the corner of the goal toward the rear line and then clear the ball from behind the goal, rather than to attempt to pass to a teammate down the field or run out to the side or down the field himself. When clearing takes place from behind the goal, the defense players must place themselves in advantageous positions. As the goalie runs behind the goal with the ball, two defense men im-

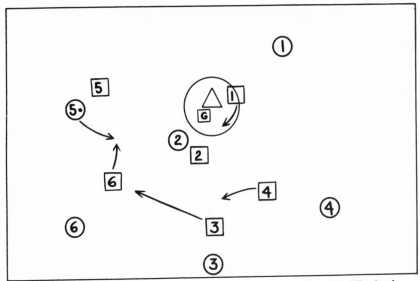

DIAGRAM 70. PICKING UP THE DODGER. ⑤ goes by 5; 6 checks him hard. 3 and 4 shift quickly to cover ⑥ and ③ respectively. 1 comes to the crease ready to play ④.

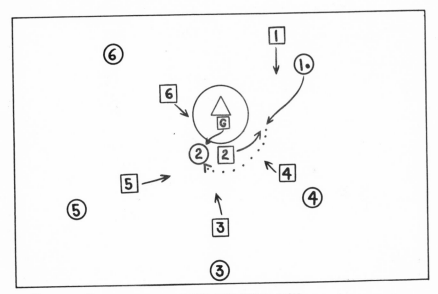

DIAGRAM 71. GOALKEEPER TAKES THE EXTRA MAN.
A. ① breaks from 1 and becomes the extra. Goalie directs 2 to take ①. ① passes to ②. Goalie takes ② as ② is about to catch the ball. 3, 4, 5 and 6 drop back toward the goal.

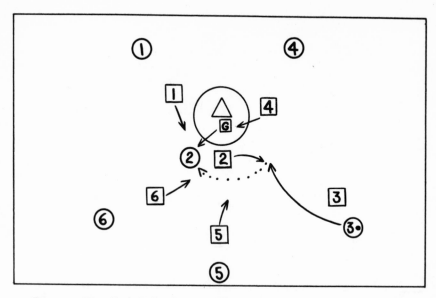

DIAGRAM 71.   B.   ③ breaks away from ③ and becomes the extra. Goalie tells ② to take ③, ③ passes to ②. Goalie takes ②. ①, ④, ⑤ and ⑥ drop back toward the goal.

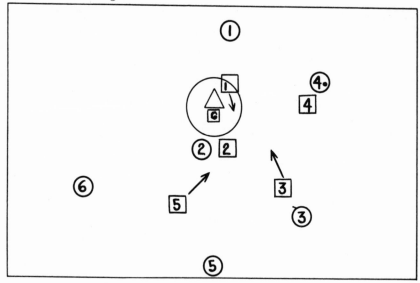

DIAGRAM 72.   ONE MAN OUT OF THE GAME.
A.   ⑥ is out of the game. ④ has the ball. ④ forces ④. ① and ③ drop back, ② covers ②, and ⑤ drops back to take ⑤ or ⑥.

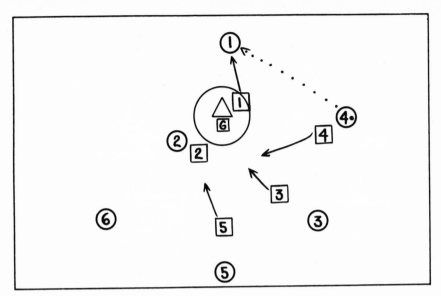

B. 6 is out. 4 forces ④, who passes to ①. 4 drops back immediately toward the goal. 1 picks up ① and forces him. 3 and 5 move in closer to the center. 2 covers ②.

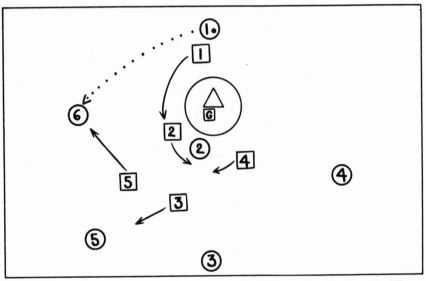

C. 6 is out. 1 forces ①, who passes to ⑥. 5 immediately plays ⑥, 3 covers ⑤ (but not too far out), 2 covers ②, and 1 and 4 come in front of the goal. *See D next page.*

129

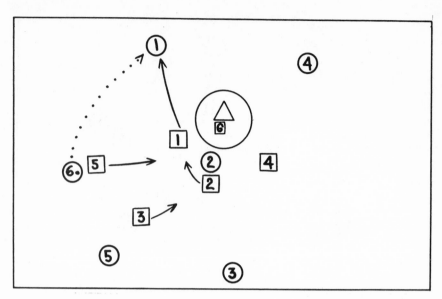

DIAGRAM 72. D. ⑥ passes back to ①. ① covers ①, ② covers ②, ④ and ⑤ move back, ready to play ④ and ⑥ respectively, while ③ plays between ③ and ⑤.

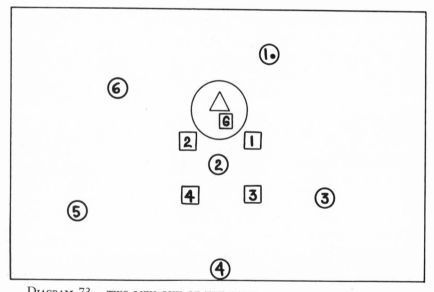

DIAGRAM 73. TWO MEN OUT OF THE GAME.
A. ⑤ and ⑥ are out. ① has the ball. ①, ②, ③ and ④ form a square in front of the goal and wait for the attack to come in to take a shot.

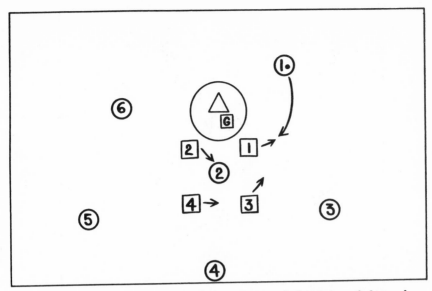

B. ⑤ and ⑥ are out. ① brings the ball around the corner of the goal.
① waits until ① is just about ready to shoot and then checks him. ②, ③
and ④ keep their positions but must be ready to check any player to
whom ① may pass as that player comes in for a shot.

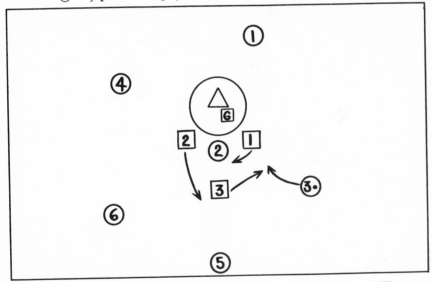

DIAGRAM 74. THREE MEN OUT OF THE GAME.   ④, ⑤ and ⑥ are
out. ③ has the ball: ①, ② and ③ arrange themselves in a triangle in front
of the goal. As ③ comes in to take a shot, ③ checks him hard, ① covers
②, and ② moves over toward ⑤. All three must stay close to the goal.

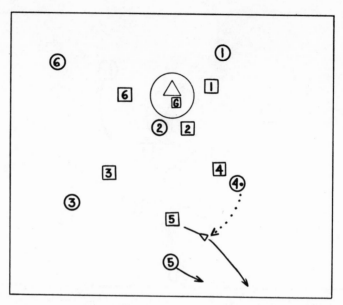

DIAGRAM 75. INTERCEPTING A PASS.   ⑤ intercepts a pass from ④ intended for ⑤ and carries the ball up the field to his own attack.

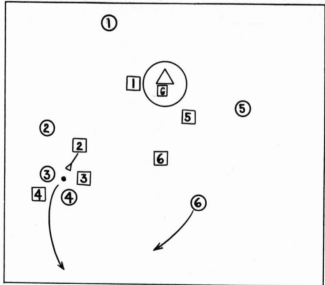

DIAGRAM 76. RECOVERING A LOOSE BALL.   ③, ③, ④ and ④ are scuffling for a loose ball. Suddenly ② crashes through the group, recovers the ball and carries it up the field to his own attack.

mediately cut back with him, each about 10 yards on either side of him. The third defense man remains in front of the goal; the midfield players break up the field—one running directly up the middle and two spreading toward the side lines. Diagram 78 illustrates the movements of these defense men. Now the goalkeeper can pass the ball up the left or right side of the field, with a short or long pass, or pass the ball along the end line to a player who clears up the field. Sometimes, after the goalie makes his first pass, the third man behind the goal is the only player open, and he receives the second pass rather than a teammate up the field. Other times, after the ball has been cleared up one side of the field, the ball carrier finds himself so covered that he must turn back, so he sends the ball behind the goal again, and a teammate clears it up the other side of the field. Diagrams 79 to 83 illustrate some of the situations that may arise in clearing from behind the goal.

It is most important, in clearing, for one of the midfield defense men to get to the center line as quickly as possible. He is in a position, then, to step over the center line in order that one of his attack teammates may cross the center line to meet an oncoming pass without being off-side (see page 15). Diagram 84 shows the value of a midfield man at the center line during a clearing play. The defense man must be alert to the situation and tell his attack teammate when to cross the center line.

No matter what situation develops, a defense man must never pass to a teammate in front of the goal when attempting to clear. Such a play gives the opposing team an opportunity to intercept the ball in close scoring territory. Diagram 85 shows how an intercepted pass results in a score for the opposition.

Under Pressure

If the defense player carrying the ball finds himself completely cornered by opposing attack players, with no teammate nearby to whom to throw the ball, he should throw a long pass to a close-attack teammate. Sometimes it is best to throw the ball just over the head of the close-attack player who is closest to the center line. Then it is up to the attack man playing near the goal to get the ball before his opponent does. Other times it is best to throw the ball on the ground directly to the attack teammate who is playing near the center line. The method to use depends upon the formation of the players who are waiting for the ball. Notice the different formations of the players waiting for the ball in Diagram 86—A and B.

Another way to get out of trouble is through the use of the toss dodge. If a defense player who has the ball is confronted by his

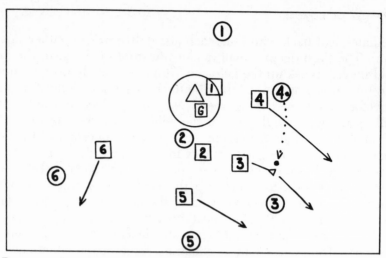

DIAGRAM 77. BREAKING INTO OPEN TERRITORY.

A. [3] intercepts the pass from (4) and carries the ball to open territory. [4] and [5] go out to assist him. [6] cuts to the opposite side of the field.

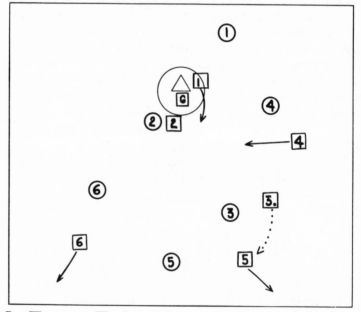

B. [3] passes to [5], who either passes the ball up the field to his attack, or carries it up if no one is open to receive a pass. [4] and [1] come back in front of goal. [6] continues up the field on the opposite side.

134

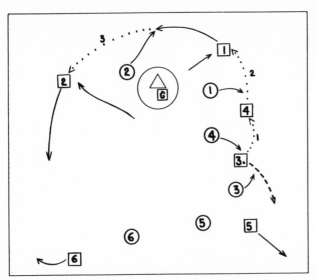

C. ③ forces ③ to turn back. He passes to ④, who in turn passes to ①.
If ② checks ①, he passes to ②. ② either passes directly to an open man,
③, ⑤ or ⑥, or runs with the ball until someone takes him. The goalie is
available as an extra man if he is needed.

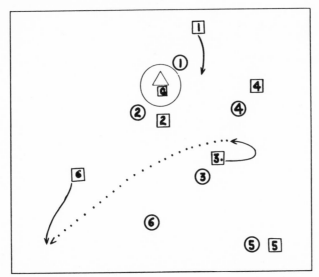

D. ③ finds ④ and ⑤ are covered. Turning, he observes ⑥ open and
passes across the field to ⑥. If ⑥ is not open, ③ goes toward ④, forcing
④ to take him and thus sets up the situation illustrated by C. There
should always be a man in the ⑥ position in the diagram. A defense player
on the opposite side from the field of action is rarely covered.

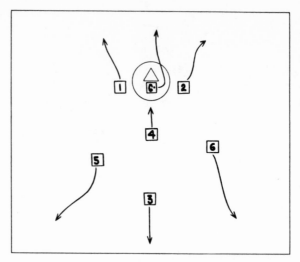

DIAGRAM 78. POSITIONS OF DEFENSE PLAYERS ON CLEARING FROM BEHIND
THE GOAL.   G , the goalie, has carried the ball behind the goal. 1 and
2 go back to help him. 4 drops back toward the crease, 3 moves out
toward the center line, and 5 and 6 break out toward the side lines. As
soon as the goalie makes his first pass, 4 breaks toward that side.

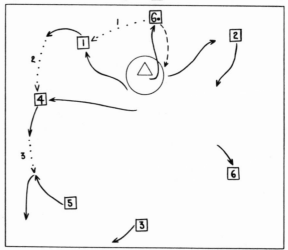

DIAGRAM 79. CLEARING WITH A PASS TO THE LEFT AND RIGHT SIDES.
A.   G passes to 1 and starts back toward his goal. 4 cuts out and
receives a pass from 1 . As this pass is made, 5 cuts back fast to receive
a pass from 4 . (If 3 or 6 are open, 4 can pass the ball to one of them
instead of to 5 .). After 1 makes his pass to 4 , both he and 2 run back
to the front of the goal.

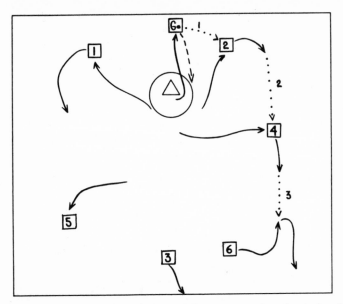

B. A situation similar to the one in A follows, except that the goalie clears to the right. ④ cuts out as the first pass is made but not until then.

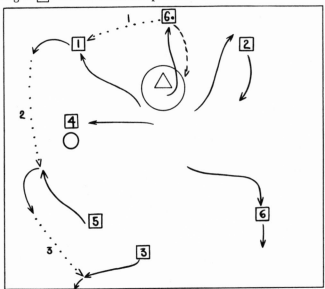

DIAGRAM 80. CLEARING WITH THE LONG PASS. Ⓖ passes to ①. ④ is covered, but ⑤ is open so ① passes directly to ⑤. ③ cuts out to receive a pass from ⑤. ⑥ stays on the far side of the field.

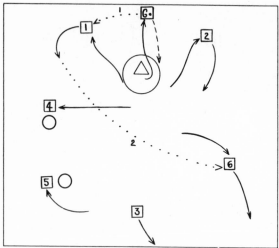

DIAGRAM 81. CLEARING WITH A PASS ACROSS THE FIELD. [G] passes to [1]. [1] observes that [4] and [5] are covered. However, [6] lifts his stick over his head to signal that he is open. [1] passes across the field to [6]. (This pass must be high, and is never made if there is any danger of interception.)

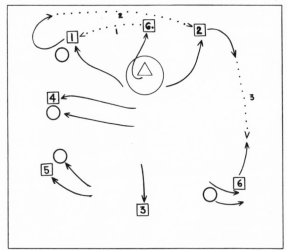

DIAGRAM 82. CLEARING WITH A PASS TO THIRD MAN BEHIND THE GOAL. The goalie carries the ball behind the goal and passes to [1]. [1] sees no one open up the field, turns and passes across the field to [2] (the third man behind the goal). [2] either carries the ball up the field or passes to [6] if he is open. (If the goalie passes first to [2], [1] becomes the third man behind the goal. A pass from [2] to [1] subsequently reaches [5] up the field.)

138

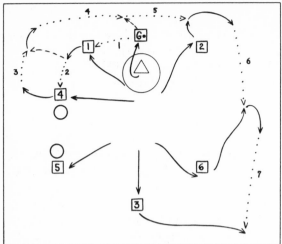

DIAGRAM 83. CLEARING BY PASS-ING TO ONE SIDE THEN THE OTHER. The goalie carries the ball behind the goal and passes to ①, who in turn passes to ④. However, ④ is covered, sees no one to pass to up the field, so turns back. ④ returns the ball to ①. ① passes to the goalie, who in turn passes to ②. ⑥ cuts back to meet the ball and re-ceives a pass from ②. ⑥ passes to ③, who carries it on down the field or passes to one of his close-attack teammates. (Sometimes ① makes his second pass directly to ② be-cause the goalie has returned to the goal. ④ must drop back in front of the goal after he passes the ball.)

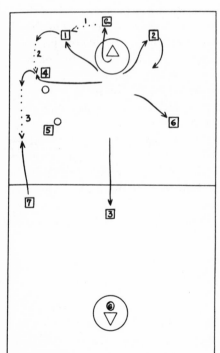

DIAGRAM 84. CLEARING TO A CLOSE-ATTACK PLAYER. Goalie passes to ①, who in turn passes to ④. ⑤ is covered, but ⑦ (a close-attack teammate) crosses the center line on ③'s signal and receives a pass from ④. (This play is also used to advantage when a loose ball is rolling near the center line.)

139

opposing attack man and no other opponent is close by, the defense player may toss the ball on the ground around the attack man, run around him, recover the ball, and carry it up the field. Diagram 87 demonstrates a method of clear similar to the pass and cut play of the attack.

Against the Zone Ride

When the ball is recovered by the defense behind the goal, the six attack men often employ the zone ride. These attack players drop back near the center line and arrange themselves in two rows of three men—the midfielders at the center line and the close-attack men 10 or 15 yards in front of them—and wait for the defense to come to them (see page 95). To clear through a zone ride, the defensive team proceeds as follows:

1. Two of the three close-attack men, who are waiting for the ball, must drop back toward the goal they are attacking. Thus they have room to come to meet any pass that is sent to them. The third close-attack man crosses to the *defensive* side of the center line.

2. The midfield men cross the center line. This gives the remaining defense men more room to operate, since their opponents must follow them or allow a four-against-three play to be established.

3. The remaining three defense men and the goalie advance *four abreast* some 10 yards apart, thereby immediately setting up an extra man. They must not play too close together, or the effectiveness of the extra man will be lost. The first pass should not be made until someone makes a move to check the ball carrier. Possibilities for passes depend upon which opponent checks the ball carrier. It would be disastrous for the defense to lose the ball in this setup, since the goalie is out of position. Diagram 88 illustrates ways of clearing through the zone ride.

PASSING TO THE ATTACK

In order to score goals, the attack must have the ball. Hence, it is most important that the defense get the ball up the field as quickly as possible. This does not mean that haste must take the place of careful, deliberate clearing.

If the ball is received by the close attack when the midfield players are not up the field, the close-attack players may employ dodges and cut and pass plays until the midfield players get up the field. Also, if a close-attack man has the ball, he passes to any extra man who may be running up the field ahead of his opponent.

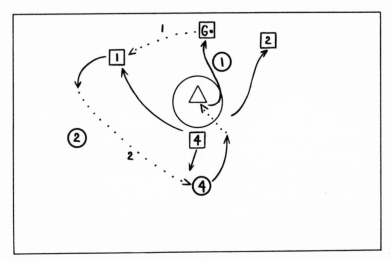

DIAGRAM 85. CLEARING INCORRECTLY. Goalie passes to ①. ④ cuts toward the center instead of toward the side line. ① makes a pass to him which is recovered by ④, who scores. Two mistakes were made: ① should never have passed the ball and ④ should have cut to the sideline.

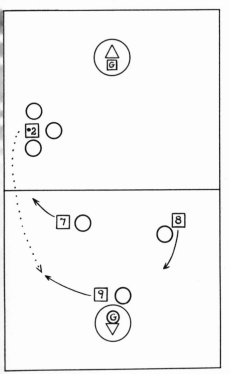

DIAGRAM 86. CLEARING UNDER PRESSURE. A. ② has the ball and is trapped by his opponents. He makes a lob pass over the head of ⑦. ⑨ must get the ball. ⑧ goes in to the crease.

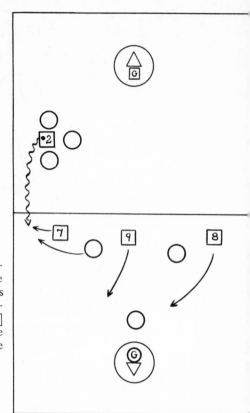

DIAGRAM 86. B. With the attack playing near the center line, ②️ throws the ball on the ground to ⑦. ⑦ either gets the ball or makes sure it goes by the defense man playing him. (For this play, ②️ must not throw the ball too hard. If he does, the opposing goalkeeper or defense player will get the ball.)

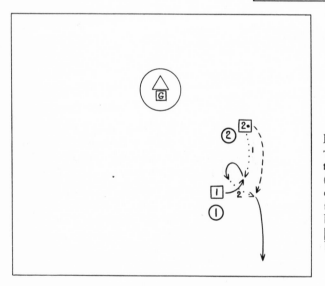

DIAGRAM 87. CLEARING, USING THE PASS AND CUT. ②️ has the ball and is being forced by ②. Although ①️ is covered, he cuts directly toward ②️. ②️ passes to ①️ and then immediately breaks up the field near him. ①️ returns the pass as ②️ goes by him.

The ball reaches attack players more quickly if it is passed rather than carried up the field. Too often a defense player with the ball chooses to run with it. He should pass at the first opportunity. The decision rests with the man with the ball. Diagram 89 shows two situations that may arise.

ZONE DEFENSE

One way to defend the goal is by means of a zone formation. With this method, each defense man has a certain *territory* for which he is responsible rather than a particular *man*. He picks up any opponent who invades his territory, or *zone*. The system of zone play requires the defense men to play close to the goal. They seldom force a ball carrier outside their territorial boundaries; therefore, they seldom play an opponent behind the goal. Diagram 90 shows the six zones that must be covered and the defense men and the goalie within their respective zones. Play is usually started from these positions. A defense player may leave his zone on occasion, particularly if he is playing the man with the ball.

To be successful, the zone defense needs an exceptionally good player to cover the crease territory ([I] in Diagram 90). This pivot man backs up any teammate playing the ball carrier and watches any opponent on the crease. He need not go much out of his territory to assist. Since the other defense men congregate more or less on the boundary of the pivot player's territory, any attack player in there can be reached by several defense men within a fraction of a second.

The zone-defense system of play has its advantages. The defense men are close to the goal, hence dodging by the attack is not too successful. If the attack man dodges by the first defense man, the pivot man can smother the dodger before he can shoot or pass. The attack finds it difficult to make a pass from one side of the goal to the other, because the scoring territory is congested with defense men who may intercept the ball. If a team has only one outstanding defense player, or if a team has one strong, fast player with mediocre stickwork but who can react quickly under pressure, the zone defense is effective. It is often used when a defense man has been ejected from the game.

The system of zone play also has its disadvantages. Any fast-moving, sharp-passing attack can confuse the defense men as they try to determine just which opponent they should play. During their uncertainty the attack may score. The zone system permits

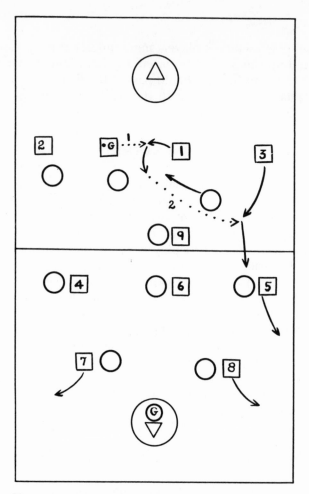

DIAGRAM 88. CLEARING THROUGH THE ZONE RIDE.

A. The midfielders and goalie advance four abreast. The goalkeeper has the ball and carries it until someone takes him. Because of the extra, one attack player has to take two men. Assume that one attack player is playing both [1] and [3], and that [2] is covered. Then the goalie makes the first pass to [1]. [1] passes to [3], who carries the ball across the center line and down the field or passes to [5] or [8], if they are available. (Notice that [9], a close-attack player, has stepped across the center line in order to make sure that [3] will not be off-side.)

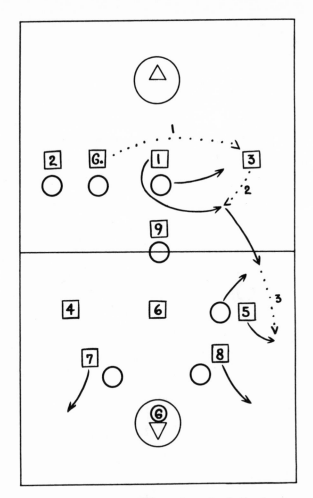

B. The goalkeeper has the ball. Assume that [1] and [2] are covered, [3] is open. The goalie passes to [3]. [1] cuts and receives a pass from [3]. [1] carries the ball down the field or passes to [5] or [8]. [9] prevents his teammate from being off-side by stepping across the center line.

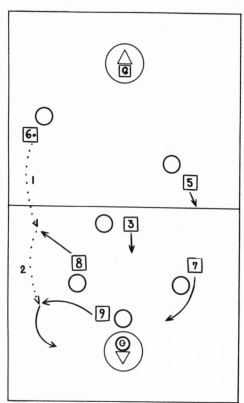

DIAGRAM 89. PASSING TO THE ATTACK.
A. A defense player, [6], has the ball. Rather than running with it, he passes the ball to [8], who is open. [8] passes to [9], who turns ready to pass to anyone who may be open. [7] goes to the crease.

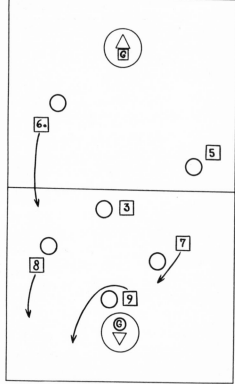

B. [6] has the ball. All attack players are covered, so [6] carries the ball up the field. [8] moves back toward his own goal as [6] comes up the field. [9] drifts to the side and [7] moves toward the goal area.

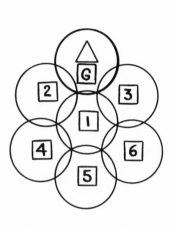

DIAGRAM 90.   ZONE SYSTEM OF DEFENSE.

the man with the ball to get in fairly close to the goal, and, if the attack can make short accurate passes, they can make close shots at the goal. If the attack players close in with their men, ready to check their opponents' sticks, they also find many opportunities for long shots. The zone system slows the game considerably because the opposing attack, if it does not know how to get through this style of defense, passes the ball around and around on the outside of the circle of waiting defense men. Nothing in lacrosse is so monotonous as this style of offense.

TWO AGAINST ONE

Many times during the game, two teammates and an opponent struggle for a ground ball. If the two teammates play together properly they should recover the ball every time; however, the third man often gets the ball. It is essential that the players be familiar with some simple system of talk and that they know exactly what is expected of them when the situation arises. This knowledge is acquired through constant practice.

When there are two against one, one player of the two must take the *man* while the other player plays the *ball*. The member of the

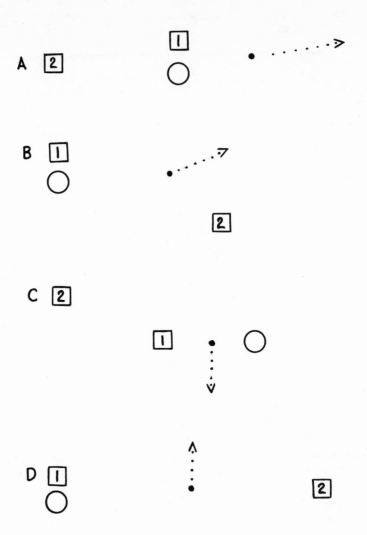

DIAGRAM 91. TWO AGAINST ONE.   In A, 2 calls, "Take the man"
since 1 may not know he is near. On hearing the command, 1 forgets
the ball and tries to keep his opponent out of the play. In B, 2 calls, "Take
the man." 2 plays the ball and 1 plays the man. In C, 2 calls, "Take the
man." He plays the ball as 1 takes the man out of the play. In D, no
command is necessary since both 1 and 2 can see each other. 1 takes
the man and 2 takes the ball. The important and necessary time to call
is when one player does not know his teammate is near enough to help him.

pair who gives the directions is the player who is in the best position to size up the situation. He signals only if he intends to take the ball. An easy command to give is "Take the man." Hearing the call, the teammate puts his entire energy into playing the man. Remember that the only time any player can use his body to prohibit a player from getting the ball is when both players are within 15 feet of a loose ball. Furthermore, as soon as the ball is lodged in the stick of any player, it is a foul to check or interfere with any other player without the ball in any way. Diagram 91 illustrates several situations where three players are involved over a ground ball.

CROSSING THE CENTER LINE

Each team must have three attack men and four defense men on their respective sides of the center line at all times. If Team A does not, then Team A is said to be *off-side*. The penalty for Team A for being off-side in case of a loose ball is to award the ball to a player on Team B. If a player on Team A has the ball when off-side is called, it is taken from him and given to a player on Team B. If Team B has the ball at the time Team A is off-side, the player on Team A who was off-side is put out of the game for 30 seconds. It is important, therefore, for the members of both teams to remain on-side. When a loose ball rolls near the center line, the nearest player to it, X, may not cross the center line to pick it up, *unless* a teammate, O, steps across the line in the opposite direction. Otherwise X will be off-side. O, in stepping across the line, keeps X on-side—maintains the proper number of players on one half of the field. Teammate O is usually far from the ball and in a position to step over the line as he calls to X to cross over and play the ball or receive the pass. Diagram 92 shows how players on the same team "exchange places" to keep the team on-side.

PICKING UP THE LOOSE BALL

A defense player while clearing, or an attack player while attempting to score, should never pick up a loose ball and then abruptly pivot and start to run in a direction not within his line of vision. There is too much danger of his being checked by an opposing player who may be directly behind him. There is danger not only of losing the ball but also of bodily injury. Whenever a player

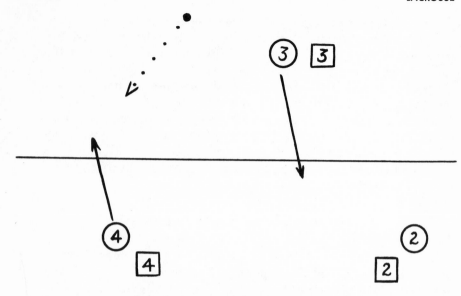

DIAGRAM 92. CROSSING THE CENTER LINE.   ③, realizing he cannot get the ball, crosses the center line, thereby enabling ④ to go after the ball without being off-side.

recovers a loose ball, he must carry it into open territory by continuing to run in a direction in which he can see clearly. (See Diagram 93.)

EXERCISES

Exercise 1 (*illustrated*)

Formation. A goalie, three defense men, and three midfield players in standard formation (one man on the crease, two men on either side, and three men in the goal area). A midfielder has the ball.

Objective. To practice clearing.

Procedure. (See Diagram 94.) A midfielder takes a shot at the goal. The goalie, ⌐G⌐, makes the stop and carries the ball behind the goal. ⌐1⌐ and ⌐2⌐ break with him, one on either side and about 10 yards from him. At the same time midfielders ⌐3⌐, ⌐5⌐, and ⌐6⌐ break out, one to the center line and the other two to the side lines. Player 4 holds his position until the goalie makes his first pass; then he cuts straight out to the ball side.

Suggestions. Have the ball cleared up first one side and then the other. Have the players exchange positions. Practice the exer-

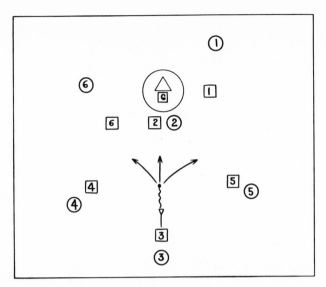

DIAGRAM 93.   PICKING UP A LOOSE BALL.

A.   [3] picks up the loose ball and continues to carry it into clear territory—follows one of the paths indicated by the arrow. Thus he sees where
he is going and avoids his opponents. Then he turns and passes the ball
up the field.

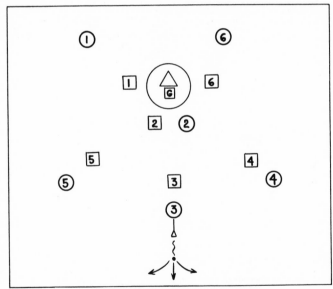

B.   (3) picks up the ball and carries it into clear territory. Even though
he may be in scoring territory he does not immediately turn back toward
his goal. His first duty is to protect the ball. To do this he runs in one of
the paths indicated by the arrow. Then he turns and passes or carries the
ball toward the goal.

151

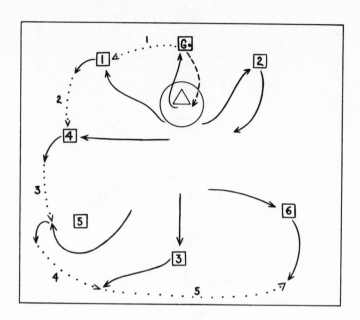

DIAGRAM 94.   EXERCISE 1.   CLEARING.

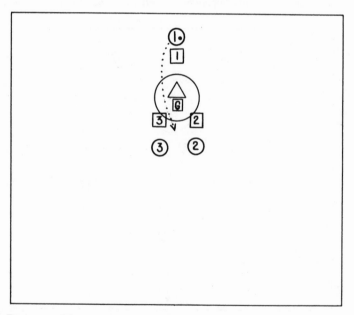

DIAGRAM 95.   EXERCISE 4.   INTERCEPTING.

152

cise a long time without an attack playing. Then have an attack
ride as the defense clears.

Exercise 2

Formation. Two columns of ten players each. One player in the
first pair has the ball.
Objective. To practice passing and throwing.
Procedure. Each pair carries the ball up the field and back, passing it back and forth between them as they run.
Variation. Have three men at a time pass the ball among themselves as they go up and down the field.

Exercise 3

Formation. Several groups of three players each. One player has
the ball.
Objective. To intercept passes.
Procedure. Two of the players play catch. The third player, sta-
tioned about 3 or 4 yards away from one of the pair, attempts to
intercept the ball as the two pass back and forth.
Suggestion. Have the players take turns at intercepting the ball.

Exercise 4 (*illustrated*)

Formation. One attack man, behind the goal, has the ball. Two
attack men play on either side of the crease in front of the goal.
Three defense men cover the attack men; two play the crease
men, with their backs to the ball. The goalie covers the goal.
Objective. To block passes and to cover sticks as passes are made
into scoring territory.
Procedure. (See Diagram 95.) ①, in possession of the ball behind
the goal, passes it to either ② or ③. ① attempts to block the
pass, and ② and ③ cover their opponents' sticks as the goalie
calls, "Check."
Suggestion. Have the players vary their positions.

8

GOALTENDING

Probably the most important position on the field is that of the goalkeeper. He must have plenty of courage, a steady eye, speed, excellent stickwork, and intelligence.

BODY AND STICK POSITION

When defending the goal, the goalkeeper always faces directly toward the man with the ball and stands about a foot in front of the goal. He crouches with legs slightly apart and holds his stick in a natural, comfortable position. As the attack passes or carries the ball back and forth, the goalie constantly shifts his position so that he always faces the ball carrier.

The goalie's stick must have a short handle so that he can easily shift it from one side of his body to the other. His hands, fairly close together, clasp the stick near the throat. This grip enables him to move the stick rapidly in any direction.

When a player shoots, the goalie must be directly in line with the path of the ball. As the ball reaches him, the face of the stick is perpendicular to the path of the ball and the goalie permits the stick to give with the ball with a slight outward twist. If the ball approaches him on the ground, he brings his legs sharply together with the heels touching and the toes pointed outward as he makes the stop (see Figure 23 A). The motion is a smooth backward slide, bringing the heels together with a click, without taking the feet off the ground. Bringing the legs together prevents a low, bad hop from going between the legs and into the goal. Keeping the feet on the ground prevents a score by an attack man who fakes high and then drops the ball on the ground at the feet of the goalkeeper.

If the ball comes in on the bounce or directly in the air, the goalie must keep the face of the stick and his body in line with the ball (see Figure 23 B). His stick gives with the ball, and he twists it slightly outward as he catches the ball.

When the ball carrier is in back of the goal, the goalie stands erect by the corner of the goal nearest the ball, about 2 feet from the goal—always facing the ball carrier. Diagram 96 illustrates the various positions of the goalie in relation to the ball.

When the ball is from 15 to 20 yards in front of the goal, the stick should be carried at a waist-high position. As the ball carrier moves in closer to the goal, the stick is gradually raised until, when he is within 10 yards of the crease, it is held near the side of the head in order to protect against a high shot.

When the attack man has the ball behind the goal, the stick should be held especially high for interceptions and in preparation for a high shot if the ball carrier should dodge around the goal for a shot.

PASSING AND CLEARING

The goalkeeper must help in the clearing and must not hesitate to come out to receive a pass. He is the extra man, the cogwheel of the clearing. As soon as he has caught the ball, he carries it out of danger. If the way is clear, the best place for him to run is straight up the field (see Diagram 97 A). Generally, however, there is an opponent on the crease, so the safest thing for him to do is to carry the ball behind the goal. From there he assists in clearing (see Diagram 97 B and pages 126 to 140).

The goalkeeper should pass the ball as soon as he can. His place is in front of the net, and he must not persist in carrying the ball until it is taken away from him. Many times he will have to run with it for a considerable distance, but he must pass the ball to an *open* teammate at the *first* opportunity.

FIGURE 23.   THE GOALTENDER.
A.   Stopping the ball with the legs.

B.   Catching the ball on a bounce.

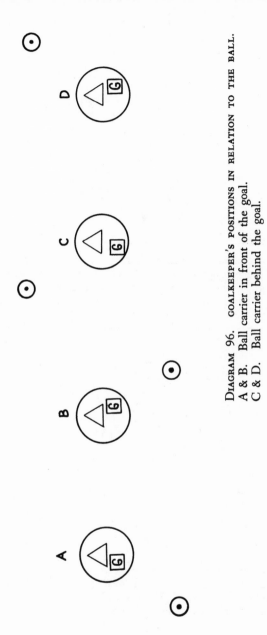

DIAGRAM 96. GOALKEEPER'S POSITIONS IN RELATION TO THE BALL.
A & B. Ball carrier in front of the goal.
C & D. Ball carrier behind the goal.

157

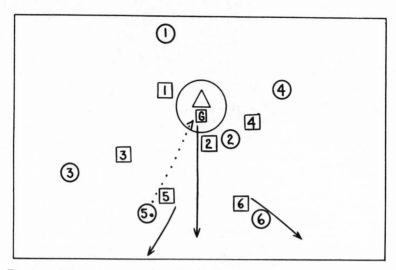

DIAGRAM 97.   GOALKEEPER CLEARING THE BALL.

A.   The goalkeeper stops a shot for goal made by ⑤. Since ②, the crease man, is out of position, the goalie carries the ball directly up the center of the field. [5] and [6] open to the right and left respectively. The goalie passes to either one as soon as he sees that one is open.

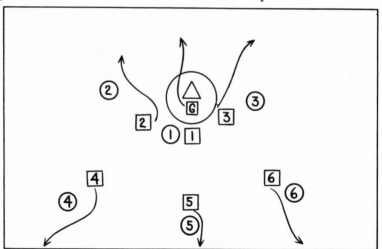

B.   The goalkeeper stops the ball, and since ① is on the crease, he carries the ball behind the goal. [2] and [3] run with him, spreading as they run. [4], [5] and [6] start up the left, center and right of the field (see Chapter 7).

PLAYING THE LOOSE BALL

The goalie should go after any loose ball that he thinks he has an even chance to recover, especially if the ball is behind the goal. However, he must not stay out of the goal in order to scrimmage with an opponent for possession of the ball. Diagram 98 illustrates when a goalie should go for a loose ball (A) and when he should not (B).

INTERCEPTING AND CHECKING

Often, by alert playing, the goalie may intercept passes near the corner of the goal. Passes made to players on the crease or to a man on the point (directly behind the goal) are the easiest to intercept. A goalie must be ready to attempt such a play, but he must be cautious and not permit himself to be drawn too far away from the net. Diagram 99 illustrates a goalkeeper's intercepting of passes.

The goalkeeper must be ready to check an open man who is about to receive a pass. He must check with lightning speed and hit the man as he is about to catch the ball. It is dangerous for the goalie to check, if the open man is too far away from the goal, since the goalie must leave his station unprotected to do so.

DIRECTING THE DEFENSE

The goalkeeper must calmly guide and direct the playing of his defense. As the attack brings the ball down the field, the goalie must tell the defense man playing the ball carrier where to check him. He must not let him play his man too far out or too close to the goal. Every time an attack makes a pass that might result in a shot for goal, the goalie calls, "Check." When he does, every defense man playing in scoring territory covers his opponent's stick tightly. The defense must learn to listen to him and to obey him. He must continually advise his defense to drop back closer to the goal, to pick up the man with the ball, to break into a clear, to hold the man with the ball, and to perform other necessary actions.

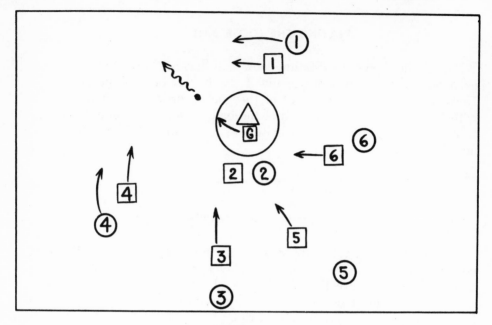

DIAGRAM 98. GOALKEEPER PLAYING A
LOOSE BALL.
A. The ball rolls free behind the goal
and the goalie leaves the goal and makes
a play for it.

TAKING AN ATTACK MAN OFF THE POINT

Defense players must not permit the ball carrier to tarry long on
the point behind the goal. He is in too good a position to make short
and quick passes. In watching him, the goalie has to keep his back
to the players in scoring territory. Hence, when the man with the
ball manages to get directly on the point, the goalkeeper and a defense man must team together to chase him away. Diagram 100
illustrates ways to do this.

PRACTICE

Following are suggestions for a coach who is training a new goalkeeper:

   1. Have him practice fundamentals—playing catch, scooping the ball
     off the ground, running with the ball, and passing—just as defense

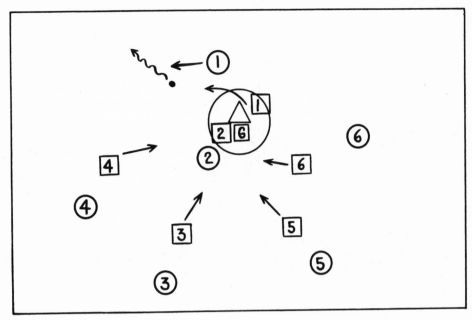

DIAGRAM 98. B. The ball rolls free behind the goal, but the goalie sees that he
has no chance to play the ball since ①
is much closer to the ball than he is.
Hence, the goalie does not leave his post.

and attack players do. He joins the others each day for this practice.

2. Have him practice stops in front of the goal with a small-faced
   stick. Throw ground balls to him, slow rollers and gentle bouncers
   with the ball bouncing just away from his feet. If he becomes
   adept with the small face, he will find it easier to handle stops with
   his own stick.

3. Have him stop the ball with his body and his legs (no stick in
   hand). Throw him an easy ball. He should develop a conscious-
   ness of stopping the ball with his body.

4. Have him, with his own stick in hand in front of the goal, stop
   shots for at least a half-hour. Vary the shots: long and short shots,
   high and low bounce shots, shots from various angles, close easy
   shots in the air at all parts of the body.

Never permit an inexperienced player to throw balls at an inexperienced goalkeeper. Neither knows how to handle the stick or
the ball well enough to practice together with the other.

A

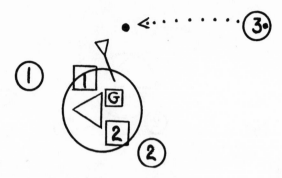

DIAGRAM 99. GOALKEEPER INTERCEPTING PASSES.
A.   The goalie intercepts a pass thrown by ③ in front of goal to ①, who is standing directly behind the goal.

B

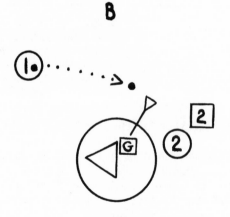

B.   The goalie intercepts a pass made from ①, behind the goal, to the crease man, ②.

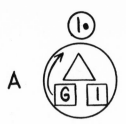

A

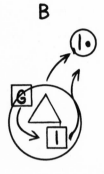

B

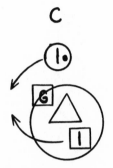

C

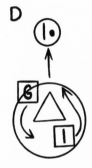

D

DIAGRAM 100. TAKING AN ATTACK MAN OFF THE POINT. In A, ①
has possession of the ball directly behind the goal. His opponent 1 is caught
at one corner of the goal. To chase ① away from this position, the goalie
starts around the other corner of the goal toward ①. B, C and D illustrate
the possibilities of ①'s first move after the goalie starts for him. As soon
as ① makes this move, 1 plays him and the goalie returns to his position
in front of the goal. In B, ① has retreated to the right of the goal and 1
immediately picks him up. In C, ① attempts to run past the goalie and
come around the left corner of the goal. 1 crosses quickly in front of the
goal and picks up ①. In D, ① drops back directly behind the goal and
1 immediately picks him up.

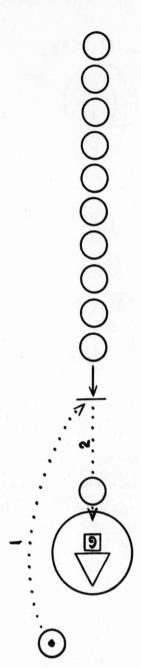

DIAGRAM 101. EXERCISE 2.

Every goalkeeper should practice for a few minutes in each goal before play is called. Teammates should send him easy shots to play. This gives the goalkeeper confidence, eases his nervous tension, and gives him the proper mental attitude for playing the game.

EXERCISES

Exercise 1

Formation. Goalie in front of the goal. One player behind the goal to back up the shots and one man with the ball in front of the goal.
Objective. To practice stopping the ball, shooting for goal, and backing up shots for goal.
Procedure. The man with the ball takes shots at the goal. The goalkeeper tries to stop all shots. The man behind the goal backs up every shot.
Suggestions. Use long, close, ground, and aerial shots from various positions in front of the goal.

Exercise 2 (*illustrated*)

Formation. A column of ten players in front of, and about 20 yards out from, the goal. One man on the crease, one behind the goal with the ball, and a goalkeeper (see Diagram 101).
Objective. To practice stopping shots, to stress accuracy in shooting, to screen, and to back up shots.
Procedure. The ball carrier makes a lob pass to the first man in the line, who receives the pass coming to meet the ball and takes a shot. The man on the crease screens the goalie from the ball and turns to play a rebound shot. After the first pass, the shooter plays the crease, the crease man becomes the feeder, and the original passer takes his place at the end of the line.

Exercise 3

Formation. One man with the ball in back of the goal, one man on the crease, and the goalkeeper in front of the goal.
Objective. To practice intercepting.
Procedure. The man back of the goal passes to the man on the crease. Goalie attempts to intercept the pass.
Suggestions. Make the passes from all possible positions behind the goal. Have the crease man move around on the crease to receive his passes at different places.

9

ADDITIONAL PLAY PATTERNS AND DRILLS; THE STAND-UP FACE-OFF

CLEARING DRILL FOR GENERAL TEAM PLAY

The purpose of this drill, illustrated in Diagram 102, is to give all ten players on a team a chance to participate, thereby giving them the experience of team play. It is important for a team to realize it must be versatile in bringing the ball up the field. Sometimes it should clear on the left side and sometimes on the right side. In this way, the riding team is compelled to vary its patterns, and this makes it easier for the defense to clear the ball. It should be understood, however, that the defense may not have time to plan on which side of the field it will clear the ball. When this situation occurs, the man with the ball must make the decision. It is still important to practice the drill on both sides of the field.

OTHER OFFENSIVE FORMATIONS

After the ball has been carried to the offensive half of the field, the attack must be ready to go into action.

Unless a four-against-three situation, or a dodge, develops during the clear, the ball should normally be taken behind the goal, preparatory to attacking the goal.

Immediately, an offensive pattern should be set up. Starting from behind the goal, the more common formations are a 2-1-3, a 1-2-3, a 2-2-2, and a 3-1-2. The most common pattern, 2-1-3, and the pattern 3-1-2 were illustrated in Diagram 58. The 1-2-3 and 2-2-2 formations are illustrated in Diagram 103.

The offense should usually be started by passing the ball around the goal and back and forth among the players. The crease men in Diagram 103, both A and B, should be constantly on the move, exchanging positions with each other.

The passes should be quick and snappy to keep the defense on the move while the attack readies itself for a pass and cut play, a screen play, a dodge, or a long shot. The cuts may come from behind the goal, from the sides, or from in front of the goal.

Someone must always be ready to back up both behind the goal and in front of the goal. This requires constant practice in order for the players to get to know what is expected of them and to anticipate what their teammates are going to do. One player may prefer a high pass as he cuts for the goal, and another may prefer a low pass. The feeder must know the various types of maneuvers his teammates will employ. If one player is an outstanding dodger, his teammates must be ready and on the alert to position themselves properly when the dodge is made. This also takes a great deal of practice.

MIDFIELD WEAVE PLAY

In Diagram 104, a pattern of play for the midfield players has been outlined. When the first phase (Diagram 104 A) has been completed, ⑤ has the ball in the middle, with ④ on his right and ⑥ on his left. This can be repeated several times with the hope of confusing the midfield defense men and getting them off-balance.

After the third or fourth weave, one of two things may be attempted: Either the middle man, with the ball, continues his break toward the goal and shoots, or, if he is right-handed, he passes to

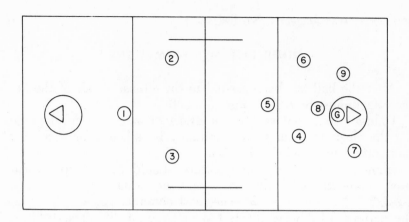

DIAGRAM 102. CLEARING DRILL. A. Team lineup.

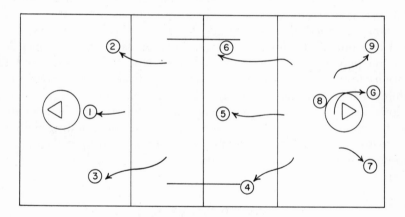

B. ⑤ is given the ball and takes a shot at his goalkeeper to start the drill. The goalie carries the ball behind the goal, and the other players immediately open up as indicated.

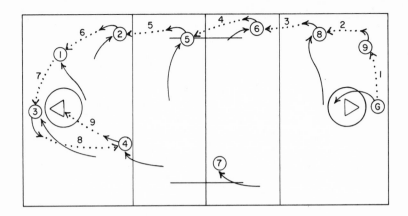

C. Ⓖ passes to ⑨, ⑧ cuts toward the side line and receives a pass from ⑨, ⑥ cuts back and receives a pass from ⑧, ⑤ cuts to the right and receives a pass from ⑥, ⑤ passes to ② while *going toward him,* ② passes to ① while moving out to his left, ③ cuts around behind the goal to receive a pass from ①, ③ moves back around the goal and passes to ④, who shoots. The ball is taken from the goal and thrown up the field to ⑦, who in turn passes it to the goalkeeper, and the drill is ready to be started over again. When repeating the drill, the ball should be cleared on the other side of the field. The drill should be practiced many times, with the players exchanging positions.

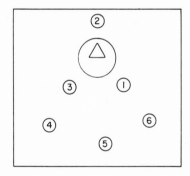

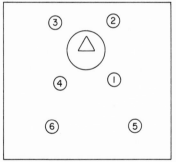

DIAGRAM 103. OFFENSIVE PATTERNS.
A. 1-2-3 formation.   B. 2-2-2 formation.

169

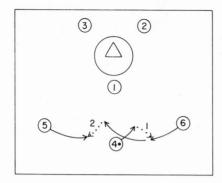 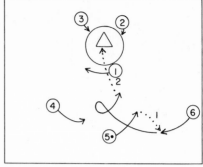

DIAGRAM 104. MIDFIELD WEAVE PLAY.

A. 4 has the ball and starts to cut in toward the goal. 6 moves toward him on the outside and receives a shovel pass from him. ⑥ now breaks toward the goal and gives a shovel pass to ⑤, who has moved toward him on the outside.

B. ⑥ cuts around in the weave and receives a shovel pass from ⑤. Instead of making his shovel pass to ④, ⑥ wheels, if right-handed, cuts on by his defense man, and takes a shot.

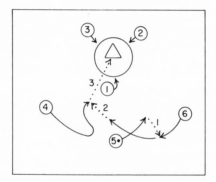

C. ⑥ cuts around in the weave and receives a pass from ⑤. ④ starts his part of the weave, but, instead of receiving a shovel pass from ⑥, he suddenly makes a break toward the goal. ⑥ passes to ④ as the latter makes his break, and ④ takes a shot at the goal.

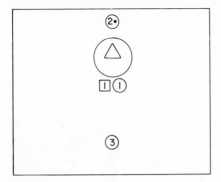 

DIAGRAM 105. CREASE-PLAY DRILLS.

A. ② is given the ball behind the goal, with ③ backing up in the center. ② and ③ do not have any defense men playing against them. The ball is passed back and forth between ② and ③ while ① makes his moves to get open. Suddenly either ② or ③ passes the ball in to ①, and 1 attempts to prevent ① from catching the ball.

B. ②, ③, and ④ have no defense against them, and ③ is given the ball. The ball is passed back and forth between ②, ③, and ④ until one of them whips the ball to ① as he maneuvers to get open. 1, of course, attempts to prevent him from making the catch.

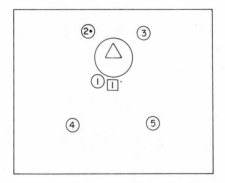

C. Four undefended players, ②, ③, ④, and ⑤, are placed around the goal. ② is given the ball, which is passed around until one of the players passes it in to ① as he works to free himself from 1. This is an excellent drill and should be practiced often during the season.

A.   Head-on view.   B.   Side view.

FIGURE 24.   THE STAND-UP FACE-OFF.

the man on his left, who cuts toward the goal. These maneuvers
are illustrated in Diagram 104–B and C. The weave play is sometimes extremely effective if the close attack replaces the midfield
in front of the goal.

CREASE PLAY

The ability of both the crease attack man and the crease defense
man to play their respective positions correctly is of vital importance
to the success of any team. Descriptions of how they should play
have already been given on pages 42 and 61, respectively. In this
section are diagrams of drills that will be beneficial to both players
(see Diagram 105).

THE STAND-UP FACE-OFF *

The stand-up face-off was suggested to the coaches of the Metro-
politan Long Island Lacrosse Association in the season of 1954 and
has been used by the high schools on Long Island ever since. This

---

* By the courtesy of William Ritch.

is also the method used by the women in their lacrosse games.

First we shall define the technique of the stand-up face-off (see Figure 24).

1. Both centers face the goal they are attacking, in a standing position.
2. The heads of the sticks are placed back to back, with the ball placed in the center and between the nettings of the two sticks. The sticks must be held motionless, with no pressure exerted until the whistle has sounded.
3. The upper arm is fully extended above the horizontal shoulder line at an angle of about 45 degrees.
4. The hand on the lower part of the stick must be pressed against the player's body.
5. The feet of each player must be placed so that the toes of both feet touch the nearest edge of the center line.
6. It is the referee's responsibility to see that there is no movement of the body, arms, legs, or crosse by either player to gain an advantage prior to the whistle starting play.
7. When the official sounds his whistle to start play, each player may attempt to direct the course of the ball by a movement of his crosse in any manner he desires.

The proponents of the stand-up face-off claim the ball is more quickly put into play, thereby speeding up the game; the danger of injury is reduced; the number of sticks broken at the face-off is reduced; and the spectators can more easily see the ball as it is put into play.

INDEX